The finishing touch

EL 0616412 9

D0230394

FT Prentice Hall

FINANCIAL TIMES

In an increasingly competitive world, we believe it's quality of
thinking that gives you the edge – an idea that opens new
doors, a technique that solves a problem, or an insight
that simply makes sense of it all. The more you know, the smarter
and faster you can go.

That's why we work with the best minds in business and finance
to bring cutting-edge thinking and best learning practice to a
global market.

Under a range of leading imprints, including *Financial Times
Prentice Hall*, we create world-class print publications and
electronic products bringing our readers knowledge, skills and
understanding, which can be applied whether studying or at work.

To find out more about Pearson Education publications, or tell us
about the books you'd like to find, you can visit us at
www.pearsoned.co.uk

The finishing touch

how to build world-class customer service

Tony Cram

**Financial Times
Prentice Hall
is an imprint of**

Harlow, England • London • New York • Boston • San Francisco • Toronto
Sydney • Tokyo • Singapore • Hong Kong • Seoul • Taipei • New Delhi
Cape Town • Madrid • Mexico City • Amsterdam • Munich • Paris • Milan

PEARSON EDUCATION LIMITED

Edinburgh Gate
Harlow CM20 2JE
Tel: +44 (0)1279 623623
Fax: +44 (0)1279 431059
Website: www.pearsoned.co.uk

Reading College Library

Order no.	
Class no.	658·812 CRA
Processed	

First published in Great Britain in 2010

© Pearson Education 2010

The right of Tony Cram to be identified as author of this work has been
asserted by him in accordance with the Copyright, Designs and Patents
Act 1988.

Pearson Education is not responsible for the content of third party internet sites.

ISBN: 978-0-273-71301-2

British Library Cataloguing-in-Publication Data
A catalogue record for this book is available from the British Library

Library of Congress Cataloging-in-Publication Data
Cram, Tony.
 The finishing touch : how to build world-class customer service / Tony Cram.
   p. cm.
 Includes index.
 ISBN 978-0-273-71301-2 (pbk.)
 1. Customer services. 2. Consumer satisfaction. I. Title.
 HF5415.5.C73 2011
 658.8'12--dc22

                            2010028202

All rights reserved. No part of this publication may be reproduced, stored in a retrieval
system, or transmitted in any form or by any means, electronic, mechanical, photocopying,
recording or otherwise, without either the prior written permission of the publisher or a
licence permitting restricted copying in the United Kingdom issued by the Copyright Licensing
Agency Ltd, Saffron House, 6–10 Kirby Street, London EC1N 8TS. This book may not be lent,
resold, hired out or otherwise disposed of by way of trade in any form of binding or cover other
than that in which it is published, without the prior consent of the publisher.

All trademarks used herein are the property of their respective owners. The use of any
trademark in this text does not vest in the author or publisher any trademark ownership
rights in such trademarks, nor does the use of such trademarks imply any affiliation with or
endorsement of this book by such owners.

The publisher is grateful to Dr Noriaki Kano for permission to reproduce Figure A8.2 and to
Sleep Country Canada (www.sleepcountry.ca) for permission to reproduce the case study on
pages 195–6.

ARP Impression 98

Typeset in Melior 9.5/13.5 by 30
Printed in Great Britain by Clays Ltd, St Ives plc

To my family

Contents

About the author

TONY CRAM IS PROGRAMME DIRECTOR at Ashridge Business School – one of Europe's leading centres for Management Development. He designs and delivers programmes on business strategy and market innovation. Tony has worked in Europe, Africa, Asia, North and South America. He is a Fellow of the Chartered Institute of Marketing.

He joined Ashridge after 20 years' experience as a manager and director in marketing, sales and general management. Tony worked initially in the motor industry and subsequently for a French company in the leisure sector. He spent 8 years with Grand Metropolitan at operating company board level, later moving to TSB Bank.

Previous books include *Customers that Count* and *Smarter Pricing*. He speaks at international conferences and seminars and has an enthusiasm for helping organisations create competitive advantage through long-term customer relationships.

Acknowledgements

MY FIRST ACKNOWLEDGEMENT goes to the many academics, authors and practitioners whose names are listed under 'Further reading' at the end of the book. In particular, I have been influenced by the thinking of Len Berry, Kathleen Seiders, Valarie Zeithaml, Mary Jo Bitner, Richard Chase, Sriram Dasu, Paul Levesque, Peter C. Verhoef, Gerrit Antonides and Arnoud N. de Hoog. I thank them for their contribution to my understanding of service encounters. Some fascinating service organisations have allowed me privileged viewpoints of their operations and I would like to say thank you to Dean Finch, Nikki Davies, Mike Hobbs, Spencer King and Ian Taylor.

Secondly, I owe a debt of gratitude to the team at the Ashridge library for extensive and creative searches to find relevant literature, examples and illustrations. Thanks to my fellow members of faculty for their support, insights and ideas especially Narendra Laljani, Lynn Lilley, James Moncrieff, Paul Pinnington, Hamish Scott and Jean Vanhoegaerden. I also appreciate the research contribution of Vicki Culpin and Shirine Voller. Chris Cram worked with me to define the scope and shape of this book. She also researched and refined examples of good practice.

Thirdly, I must thank the editorial team at Pearson Education, including Liz Gooster and Martina O'Sullivan for their encouragement, well-founded advice and positive enthusiasm. Working with them has been a good experience.

Finally, despite all the teamwork, advice and support, the views expressed and the mistakes are entirely my own.

A rising crescendo

The whistle sounds at the end of a football match. Imagine you are leaving the ground. Which is the better feeling: when your team scored the winning goal in the first five minutes of the game?

Or the last five minutes?

Scoring the winning goal in the first five minutes gives a satisfactory result, but it's not a game to remember. Rather, the exhilaration and excitement of a strong finish turns a good experience into a great one.

The first line of a joke captures your attention, but the memorable part is the punch line. A classic novel has that final twist to reward the reader. A film director focuses on building the plot to a powerful climax. The secret of success: a five-star finish.

This secret applies to service provision. It should be obvious, but does it happen? Don't be like the airline, spending money and attention on the in-flight service, only to leave customers alone and bewildered in the baggage reclaim hall, fearing the final letdown.

Much service thinking involves an analytical approach. We label this as 'left-brain thinking' because logic depends on the left hemisphere of the brain. Service managers calibrate and measure the available statistics – call analysis, speed of response, conversion ratios. These aspects are always important to deliver satisfactory service. However, to go beyond 'satisfactory' and excel, we must also call on the emotional connections. These occur in the right hemisphere of the brain. This is where feelings trigger positive perceptions.

A great service experience happens in the customer's mind. So, great service comes from understanding the actions, words and signals that place positive impressions in the customer's mind. It means managing the cues that influence mental judgements at each point.

Begin well. Build the momentum. And above all manage perceptions to a rising pitch, culminating in the grand service finale. At the end of a live concert, the audience is crying, 'Encore!' Everyone is buzzing, eager to enthuse to others. They want more. You can achieve the same in a service experience.

The finishing touch will make your customers feel positive.

The finishing touch will bring them back to buy more.

The finishing touch will make them eager to promote your service to others.

This book will help you to deliver the finishing touch.

part

1

Prologue

More service, less satisfaction – the service context

Since the 1960s the service economy of developed countries has grown considerably in the areas of distribution, hotels and restaurants, transport, storage and communication, business services, finance and public sector services. In the UK, over a 20-year period, services have grown at an average annual rate of 2.6% – almost four times the rate of manufacturing growth (Julius and Butler, 1998). According to British government statistics, services now represent 74% of the UK gross domestic product (GDP).

In the USA, the service sector accounts for 80% of economic activity. Whereas 30% of Americans worked in manufacturing in 1950, fewer than 15% work there currently. According to the US Bureau of Labor Statistics, the US has more choreographers (16,340) than metal casters (14,880), and more people earning their living shuffling and dealing cards in casinos (82,960) than running lathes (65,840). There are almost three times as many security guards (1,004,130) as machinists (385,690).

> the service sector now represents over 70% of employment in the European Union and is growing annually

In most developed countries, service accounts for 60–75% of GDP. The service sector now represents over 70% of employment in the European Union and is growing annually. The service sector also tends to recover faster than manufacturing industry after recession.

In India, the service sector accounts for 52% of GDP. In December 2009, the Chinese National Bureau of Statistics revised the added value of its service sector for 2008 to 13.13 trillion yuan from the previous 12.05 trillion yuan. The service sector accounted for 41.8% of the country's economy, up from 33% in 2004. This compares with 46% for manufacturing and 13% for primary industries.

Manufacturing businesses are finding revenue and profit growth through adding services to their range. A washing machine has insurance sold with it. Amazon.co.uk has extended from selling books, DVDs and other products, to DVD rental with club members paying a monthly fee. Farmers are converting barns into leased business units. Industrial equipment suppliers are adding packages of service, maintenance, inspection and support. Professional services are a $3 trillion industry worldwide.

You can buy a car, a computer or a shirt for less money today than each cost in 2000. But when you service that car, you will find that the hourly rate is moving firmly in the other direction. The computer may cost less but the IT support services cost more each year. The shirt is inexpensive but the laundry bill is rising. Hair shampoo comes cheap, hairdressers come dear. Economists explain that we have deflation in many categories of goods and inflation in service provision costs.

So services are becoming more prevalent, more significant as a sector of the economy and more valuable.

Lagging satisfaction

Yet despite this dramatic growth in the service sector, customer satisfaction lags product satisfaction. The annual *Service in Britain* survey from ASR and Research Now tracks customer service for all major UK service industries. Their findings consistently show that half of all consumers surveyed think that customer service standards in Britain are declining, whilst only one in six believe that standards are improving. According to the American Customer Satisfaction Index, perceptions of quality for services have been consistently lower than those of products throughout the ten years that the index has been compiled (Figure 1.1).

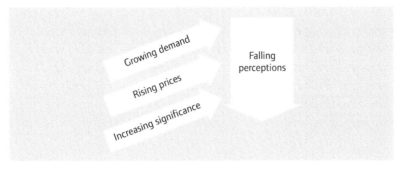

FIGURE 1.1 Rising demand, falling perceptions

At the same time, it is true that service brands face the challenge of increasingly demanding customers. Moira Elms is a board member at PricewaterhouseCoopers (PwC) with responsibility for brand, communications and experience. Speaking to *The Marketer* (Croft, 2006), she said that clients are looking for 'absolute consistency of service'. This applies even though the clients will be dealing with many different people within PwC. As a response to this challenge, PwC propounds the concept of 'one firm' as a pillar of their corporate vision. This is briefed to all employees as a common set of behaviours across PwC. In particular, the aspiration is consistently to share the knowledge of their extensive firm network to the benefit of clients.

Barriers to overcome

> service offerings are intangible and may be difficult to conceptualise

Service offerings are intangible and may be difficult to conceptualise. They are frequently customised and modified for each occasion or customer. They may, as Moira Elms described, be labour intensive and involve many different individuals collaborating to deliver the service experience. This human factor is often a key requirement for achieving high levels of appreciation. There is a human dimension to the interpretation of customer needs and customers are often involved in the process through dialogue and interaction. For instance, an architect will need to ask questions about the requirements and preferences. The quality of the dialogue will influence the effectiveness of the building design. In some sectors, such as healthcare and restaurant dining, one patient or guest may even have a bearing on the experience of their fellows. Finally, giving excellent service is difficult because the perception of 'excellence' happens in the customer's mind.

A profitable prize

Providing good service is difficult. Yet it matters to customers. Competitors are also struggling with achieving excellent service. Hence, the ability to deliver consistently superior service is one of the rare sustainable competitive advantages. Valarie A. Zeithaml and Mary Jo Bitner offer two commercial benefits of good service quality in their book *Services Marketing* (2003):

1 Offensive: attracting more and better customers.

2 Defensive: customer retention.

Offensive effects involve market capture, market share, reputation and the ability to charge a price premium. The Profit Impact of Marketing Strategy (PIMS) research is a multi-company, multi-year study. A report by strategy expert Bradley T. Gale, using PIMS data as evidence, shows that companies offering superior service have achieved higher market share growth and, in addition, gained the financial benefits of increased market share, a premium price, lowered costs and less rework. Businesses rated in the top 20% of competitors on relative service quality had on average an 8% price premium over their competitors (Gale, 1992).

Defensive effects involve greater customer loyalty and a lower level of churn or turnover of customers. This can contribute to profitability in six ways:

1. **Amortising customer acquisition costs** Lost customers must be replaced and this is expensive in acquisition costs, set-up costs and the initial lower margin that is typical of new customers. Loyalty experts Reichheld and Sasser (1990) have calculated that the longer a company keeps a customer, the more profitable that customer tends to be.

2. **Increasing value of purchases** Satisfied customers buy more. This comes from customers buying across the range, buying more frequently, upgrading, and from gaining a larger share of the customer's spend in the category.

3. **Reducing costs to serve** Greater customer knowledge enables the company to reduce costs to serve established customers. Payment performance is better and demand patterns are understood so that resourcing can be optimised and fewer errors made.

4. **Gaining market knowledge** Loyal customers share their market knowledge with their suppliers. They give feedback, and make complaints and suggestions. They provide competitor data. Their purchases can reveal burgeoning trends.

5. **Achieving a premium price** Well-served customers may pay a premium price. They are less price-sensitive because price is not the only issue in their decision to do business with a supplier. Zeithaml and Bitner (2003) cite the aggregate and rock supplier, Graniterock, 'achieving a 30% price premium; in a commodity business they benefit from an off-hour delivery and 24-hour self-service that is superior to competitors'.

6. **Recommending to potential customers** Satisfied customers recommend. Referrals can be spontaneous, indirect through client listing or even prompted in the form of testimonials.

For all these reasons, success with service can create a significant commercial advantage.

Service quality dimensions

The key question is: how do you provide highly rated customer service? The first step is to establish the criteria that customers use to determine good service quality. Research by service experts Parasuraman, Zeithaml and Berry (1988) indicates that customers assess service quality across five specific dimensions:

1. **Reliability** Ability to perform the promised service dependably and accurate.

2. **Responsiveness** Willingness to help customers and provide prompt service.

3. **Assurance** Employee knowledge and courtesy and their ability to inspire trust and confidence.

4. **Empathy** Caring, individualised attention given to customers.

5. **Tangibles** Appearance of physical facilities, equipment, personnel and written materials.

Of these five dimensions, the first factor – reliability – has consistently proved to be fundamental. Every business needs to understand their customers' expectations of reliability. Failure to provide the core service that customers think they are buying is fundamental.

To attain performance reliability, companies use process models. These models analyse service for variability, just as products are checked at the end of a production line. It is high on analysis and focused on performance consistency. Service standards are set. Monitoring mechanisms measure waiting time against targets, adherence to delivery time slots, invoice adjustments, inbound phone calls abandoned against targets. Best practice processes are established. For example, following customer demands, the British Standards Institute launched ISO 10002 in 2004 to provide an assessment system for customer complaints management.

> companies analyse feedback to identify elements that disappoint customers

Companies analyse feedback to identify elements that disappoint customers. They redesign processes to minimise or eliminate these so-called 'dissatisfiers'. For instance, customers dislike litter and graffiti in public places, so service standards have been set for new UK rail franchise operators to define the size for a discarded object above which it will be classified as litter and the minimum number of such pieces there may be in a given area.

Naturally consistent reliable performance is obviously better than variable and random performance. Expectations are set and measured. You can minimise disappointment.

But something is missing

Yet, there is more to reliability than simply avoiding disappointment.

For one thing, if service is commoditised in order to remove disappointing experiences, there is a danger that this will also squeeze out the individuality that can provide a bonus to customers. There is a 'one-size-fits-all' formula for success. Call centre agents for a leading UK bank systematically advise phone-bank customers that instructed payments will only be made if the customer still has funds available in their account on the date of the payment. The same distrustful vocabulary is applied to both an exemplary customer with a 40-year credit history and their worst customer. Retail checkout assistants obey company policy by wishing every customer 'Have a nice day!' Yet in practice they spare the people that they know personally – ironically these are the people they might wish to have a nice day!

Secondly, the standard service removes the negative and ensures that customers are not disappointed, but this still leaves scope for creating a positive experience. Customers love good news, a good feeling, an uplifting experience, a pleasant surprise or an unanticipated bonus. Adding something positive is the key to achieving a highly rated customer service.

Performance + perception

Success in service is partly answered by delivering a reliable performance to the level that the customer expects. But there is more to it than this. Let us return to the critical concept that the perception of service excellence exists in the customer's mind. We must therefore understand the evaluation processes that customers go through. We need to explore the levers for influencing those perceptions. How can we act to engage the mind of the customer? What factors create positive feelings about service encounters?

Our objective is fourfold (see Figure 1.2):

1 To satisfy the customer with the service.

2 To ensure that the service experience is noted and appreciated.

3 To encourage customers to return, providing future business.

4 To move customers to recommend our service to others.

| Service satisfaction | Service appreciation | Customer retention | Service recommendation |

FIGURE 1.2 Service objectives

Let us work back from the desired end result. If your aim is to have the customer in the mindset to recommend you and return, by the end of the encounter, what science must you apply to achieve this kind of behaviour? How does this translate to a relatively standard service like air travel, or to a more individual experience like a medical procedure? Can the rules apply to professional services?

Overturning old ideas

New service research is overturning the old paradigm that stressed a strong start and consistent performance within the encounter. A new direction of thinking for the twenty-first century was set by Hansen and Danaher (1999), asserting that 'a build-up to a strong ending results in a higher perceived service quality'. Consideration must be given to the high points and the downers that add texture and emotional depth to the service experience. Research by Verhoef, Antonides and de Hoog (2004) concluded that 'Managers should be aware that satisfaction is not created solely by the average quality of the events in the service process. Satisfaction can be further enhanced with the provision of a positive peak experience.' For a truly positive experience the emotional value must increase during the encounter. The winning approach is to manage perceptions to a rising upward trajectory. This means: begin well, build the momentum and manage perceptions upwards to end with a strong finishing touch.

> for a truly positive experience the emotional value must increase during the encounter

My research and experience across various service sectors confirms that the answer is to understand the customer's emotional journey. Envisage the service encounter as a drama. Grove and Fisk (2001) explored the potential for dramatising the service experience in research published in 1992 and 2001. They believe that, like a playwright, the designer of a service experience is dedicated to 'impression management', considering the setting, the actors and the backstage support in order to please the audience.

I have identified eight acts that create the drama of a successful service experience:

Act 1: **Preconceptions** This is the preview of the drama. Communications must attract new users and re-attract previous users to the service with an offer that is tempting, attractive and inviting, but realistic. Avoid over-promising – presenting an exaggerated portrayal of the service leads to under-delivery and disappointment. I will show how to find ways to pitch the offer so that the expectations created can be met. This act is all about expectation management and we will use all four forms to set the right preconceptions.

Act 2: **First impressions** This is the first contact. I will explain how to manage the initial greeting successfully – there is only one chance to make a first impression. I will put forward the ingredients of signalling and cues from the tangible elements of the service. I recommend a departure from one-size-fits-all, identifying instead which customers need an induction, which require a reminder and which can steer themselves through the process.

Act 3: **Building trust** This step normally takes time. Trust is confidence in the future and it grows over a period of time with consistently appropriate behaviour. I will find ways to accelerate this process with proven trust-building principles. Time means risk with today's fickle customers.

Act 4: **Reality check** In this act, I address the awkward or less pleasant parts to the experience, queuing for example. I illustrate how best to manage these moments of risk. These moments must be designed to occur early in the process to reserve ample time to restore the upward trajectory.

Act 5: **Something individual** This act is about making customers feel important. This is a key stage in lifting perceptions. When the call-centre agent or retail assistant deploys the same vocabulary and approach towards every customer, she downplays customer individuality. Yet individuality is enormously precious to customers. I spell out six ways to make the customer feel important.

Act 6: **Service recovery** This act is about delivering a winning recovery when problems arise. Remember that the most wonderful words a customer can hear (aside from their own name) is the confident phrase, 'I can fix that'. I have ways to deal with angry customers, how to turn a problem to advantage and list the ten steps of a world-class service recovery.

Act 7: **Service innovation** The focus here is to build the next service experience to exceed the current one. The rising trajectory must occur between encounters as well as during a single experience. I have a blueprint to learn from customers, observing for insight, so that we can build better and better offerings.

Act 8: **The finishing touch** This is the grand finale. How can we leave the customer wanting more, eager to tell the world about the great experience? I will tell you the winning ways to close a phone call, to finish a meeting, to conclude a consulting assignment, to discharge from a hospital stay, to arrive at the end of a rail journey. As Chase and Dasu (2001) wrote in their *Harvard Business Review* paper, 'the ending matters enormously'.

The structure of this book is based on these eight acts. I show how to manage the customers' experience so that everything points to a positive outcome in a way that is memorable and evocative. Finishing on a high note will leave customers eager to recommend your service to others and fully intent on returning next time they need this service.

Measuring feelings: the satisfaction curve

You aim to manage the customers' perceptions to achieve an upward trajectory of emotions.

> you aim to manage the customers' perceptions to achieve an upward trajectory of emotions

How will you measure this? Nineteenth-century economists calculated happiness or utility as the sum of good feelings minus bad, arguing that human activity was based around the pursuit of pleasure and the avoidance of pain. Francis Edgeworth (1881) looked forward to the invention of the *Hedonimeter*, describing it as 'a psychophysical machine' that would record the ups and downs of a man's feelings just as a thermometer might plot his temperature. Today, according to *The Economist* (2006a), this science of *hedonimetrics* is possible with a combination of brain scans of the left forebrain, measurement of smiling through contraction of the orbicularis oculi face muscles and simple self-reporting.

A satisfaction curve represents the customers' evolving perceptions. Imagine you have a hedonimeter reading of your customers as they go through your service encounter, what shape should this satisfaction curve follow?

A simple time-based satisfaction curve represents on a graph the customer's changing mindset as he or she progresses through the service experience (see Figure 1.3). The vertical scale indicates positive or negative perceptions, the horizontal axis denotes time and the black line shows the rise and fall of the customer's feelings towards the service.

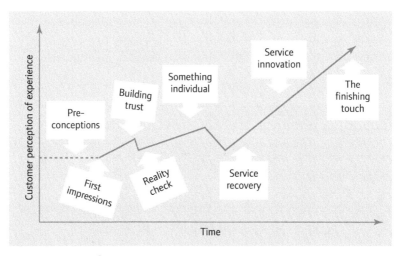

FIGURE 1.3 Satisfaction curve – service experience

The aim is to move the customer's feelings upwards over time, finishing in the highest possible point, leaving them positively minded, eager to recommend to others and ready to become loyal repeat buyers.

Crafting the service value proposition – internal foundations

The stage must be set before the drama can begin. This chapter lays down the foundations for good service. Succeeding chapters will show how to build on these foundations to rise all the way to the finishing touch.

> the value proposition is the promise you make that attracts and retains customers

The service value proposition is the starting point. It is the deal that will appeal. Specifically, the value proposition is the promise you make that attracts and retains customers. And when you have defined your offer to customers, you need strategies to deliver on this promise, every time. These are your service capabilities.

Customer value

Market success comes from offering specific customers a clear combination of benefits and price that they will find attractive. Brands create value for customers by developing products and services that customers need, and surrounding them with positive associations. Champagne, for example, is a pleasant sparkling white wine, surrounded by connotations of success and celebration.

In his book, *Delivering Profitable Value*, Michael J. Lanning (1998) defined value as 'a deliberate combination of precise benefits and price that is targeted to a specific group'. From the customer's perspective, it is an appealing set of benefits (including emotional associations) at an acceptable price level. The statement summarising this targeted offer is called a value proposition. This statement is particularly important in a service business where good service depends on the interplay of everyone in the company. When every employee understands what you are offering, to whom and how much it is worth, then their part in delivery can be clear. The value proposition pulls together and focuses the internal efforts to deliver the deal reliably and consistently (see Figure 2.1).

FIGURE 2.1 Value proposition

The three core elements of the classic value proposition, target customer group, precise benefits and defined price level, relate to service businesses as well as product brands. However, there are challenges to the service business:

▌ **Target group – the variety challenge** Where a product brand can sell successfully to many different types of buyers, the service brand is likely to be more successful with homogenous buyers whose needs are somewhat similar. Employees will find it easier to serve customers with common needs and expectations. Where service is delivered in a public environment such as an aeroplane or a restaurant, distinctly different customers may be at odds with each other.

▌ **Precise benefits – the consistency challenge** Where the product proposition delivers pre-manufactured benefits, the service brand must reproduce the same benefits for each customer in real time.

▌ **Defined price level – the value challenge** Where the product brand often has a price list, the service brand is more likely to offer prices that vary by customer, by time of day, time of year or time of booking.

So how does the service brand face this challenging environment? I will look at the three aspects in turn and then identify an important additional dimension.

Which customer?

Some service operations, such as healthcare, utilities and public sector organisations, have obligations to provide universal service. Most private sector service providers on the other hand will prefer to focus on homogenous groups of customers whose needs they can understand and meet. For instance, a consumer service will choose to focus more precisely on target segments, such as an interior design company targeting high-income groups, or a paint-ball activity company aiming for outgoing social groups. Within business-to-business, a professional services firm might aim to serve small and medium-sized enterprises. There are significant advantages for service providers who achieve homogeneity of customers served:

1. Understanding needs is easier where most customers have a similar pattern of requirements.

2. Spotting emerging trends is more productive when a new request from one customer relates to the emerging needs of other customers.

3. Training staff is easier where customer expectations follow a predictable course.

4. Homogenous groups may be more harmonious when cross-customer contact arises. For example, hotels specialising in holidays for senior citizens will discourage families with teenagers who play boisterous water-games in the swimming pool.

These advantages translate into better growth prospects, higher levels of customer retention and lower staff training costs, all of which point to potentially greater profitability. Table 2.1 shows one approach to customer targeting.

TABLE 2.1 Value proposition – defining target customers

	Current position	Future target
What is our customer mix?		
Which categories and types of customer do we wish to attract?		
Which types of potential customer will we discourage?		

Once the target customers are identified, the service company directs communications and incentives at the interests of the potential customers. In addition there may be techniques to dissuade customers outside the desired group. For example, the University of Surrey holds open days for potential undergraduates. The University's point of difference is a career approach and their close links with business through an outplacement year. A student wearing a suit and tie delivers the presentation. His words and style will attract career-orientated students and discourage the late-night party animals.

Or picture a large group of teenagers congregating in a shopping centre, not buying things themselves and obstructing regular shoppers. Mall managers have experimented with classical music through loudspeakers. The sound is acceptable to older shoppers but discourages such groups of younger people from hanging around.

Long-term customers are more attractive to a business than one-off buyers. This is especially important when the particular service calls for a considerable degree of assessment, training or customisation. These costs of acquisition can make short-term customers unprofitable. Commercial insurance companies may screen out customers who have a track record of changing suppliers regularly, because the long-term investment in building up knowledge and developing a relationship would not be paid back by a short-term customer.

Which price?

The pricing of services is a challenging area. The following factors need to be considered in setting out a price position and price structure:

1. **Price indicates quality** Services are intangible products, implying that customers may not be able to judge quality before consumption of the service. Therefore they may use price as an indicator of quality, comparing two providers.

2. **Price level sets expectations** Higher prices for services may set expectations of personal service and lower prices may lead consumers to assume that there will be a degree of self-service.

3. **Price impacts on demand** Service providers therefore use price as a mechanism to manage capacity, raising it to limit surplus demand at peak times and reducing it to stimulate business in quieter periods.

4. **Price structure stimulates usage** For example, those customers buying a package a long time in advance with a credit card are less likely to show up to a sports game or a cultural event than a late cash buyer of a single event. This knowledge can be used to influence attendance and therefore consumption of other items such as programmes and refreshments.

5. **Prices can be matched to segments** Price discrimination may be applied to achieve higher prices from segments that value the service more highly. For example, hair stylists for women charge more than men's hairdressers (except in Sweden where gender discrimination outlaws this). Airlines are beginning to surcharge 'persons of size' who need to occupy two seats. Some of these segment prices are accepted whereas other segment prices cause customer conflict.

6. **Price influences customer behaviour** Pricing can be used to help customers behave profitably, for example by surcharging wastage.

The chosen price incorporates customer perceptions, competitive differentiation and company objectives in order to attract customers, defend against rivals and secure a profitable long-run return.

Which benefits?

The customer compares the benefits available with the affordability of the price and then decides whether a service represents acceptable value. Value is partly a mathematical calculation and partly a perception in the mind of the customer. Services differ from products in a significant way: where the product proposition delivers pre-manufactured benefits, the service brand must reproduce the same benefits for each customer in real time.

> the service brand must reproduce the same benefits for each customer in real time

Service encounters go beyond simply *what* is done. Yes, customers judge services by the technical effectiveness of the service workers. But research into services shows that they also consider the *manner* in which it was done. Grove and Fisk (2001) identified this double target in their work on 'service theatre'. They write, 'the dentist, hotel clerk and educator are assessed on how well they perform regarding the outcome of their effort (for example a filled cavity, properly assigned room and information learned, respectively) and the manner in which it was done (for example the concern showed, the courtesy displayed and the responsiveness demonstrated)'.

With a service brand, the benefits go beyond the service performed to include some significant intangible elements: reassurance, convenience, peace-of-mind, a relaxing or stimulating experience. With scope for different customers to feel differently, there is a need to manage the benefit communication. This encompasses defined service promises that may be described in advertising or be specified in a service guarantee, and are likely to cover the functional service performed. In addition, there are implicit service promises, or expectations of customers. It is important to understand and influence the implicit expectations that are created through the way service staff behave, through the cues given by pricing and through signals given by the tangible parts of the process.

In what way?

The service value proposition needs a distinctive behavioural aspect. It is a deliberate combination of precise benefits and price targeted at a specific group and *delivered in a particular manner*, as in Figure 2.2. The brand then focuses on conveying this to users consistently at every touch point.

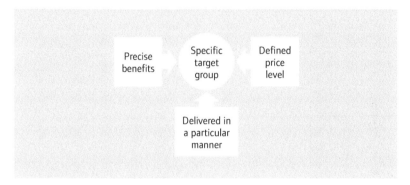

FIGURE 2.2 Service value proposition

A clear way to envisage this is to describe the service delivery with a unique behavioural adverb. Whereas adjectives encapsulate product brands, service brands are often better described by adverbs indicating the way a service is performed. For example, the distinctive character of an HMV store selling DVDs, CDs and computer games is that the service is delivered *knowledgeably*. Staff members are chosen for their individual expertise in film, music genres and computer games. They make this knowledge accessible to customers through advice, recommendations and answers to questions.

Choose the dimension for outperformance

A brand comes to life through its focus on one or two key dimensions. It cannot be number one on every attribute. The best service brands choose where they plan to outperform all others. What particular way will you choose to deliver good service? This connects with customer needs, and involves selecting one attribute for primary focus. The essence is the adverb you choose to inform all customer contact. This defines the final impression to be left with a customer.

Kwik-Fit, the leading automotive service operator with 2300 service points across Europe, focuses on behaving *reassuringly*. Historically the reputation of the automotive after-market has been tarnished by back-street mechanics exploiting the ignorance of motorists. Kwik-Fit has worked to counter this by developing and training staff to deliver absolute reliability in an open and transparent manner. For example, when Kwik-Fit replace a pair of shock absorbers, they will offer to keep the old parts, so that they might be refitted should the customer feel – after driving with the new shock absorbers – that the job was unnecessary and the new parts have made no difference. The offer is almost never invoked and in fact is designed to leave the customer feeling reassured.

Another example is Prêt a Manger, the leading sandwich retailer, which focuses on behaving *naturally*. The ingredients are natural and so is the service approach. McDonald's never uses the word 'clean' in advertising, but cleanliness is a strong subconscious need of the parents whose children enjoy visiting McDonald's. Judging from the attention staff pay to mopping floors and wiping tables in McDonald's restaurants around the world, perhaps '*hygienically*' might be their adverb. Marriott Hotels behave *hospitably* to their guests – customers are always referred to as guests, and treated as such. Consulting firm Accenture aims to respond to clients *innovatively*, endeavouring to finalise any piece of customer contact with an innovative flourish. Each of these organisations has its own interpretation or definition of what 'good service' means. Delivering consistent service adverbs is far more challenging than replicating product adjectives.

Choose your definition of good service as a style in which you will operate. What you see is what you get – *be* distinctive rather than *saying* you are distinctive. Act in consistent ways. Success in service brands is less about advertising and more about actual behaviour. It comes from placing the same feeling in the mind of the customer on every occasion. Seek creative ways to extend this style to every aspect of the customer contact, with particular attention to the closing moments. A clear value proposition makes it possible to determine the internal service capability needed to deliver the benefits consistently.

People deliver service

In their pioneering work, *Service Breakthroughs*, Heskett, Sasser and Hart (1990) identified the importance of internal service quality. Organisations wishing to deliver service quality to *external* customers must begin with serving the needs of *internal* customers. They called this the service profit chain:

1. Internal service quality drives employee satisfaction.
2. Employee satisfaction leads to employee retention and productivity.
3. Employee retention/productivity enables high value service.
4. High value service results in customer satisfaction.
5. Customer satisfaction leads to customer loyalty.
6. Customer loyalty produces profit and growth.

Profit and growth derive primarily from customer loyalty, which is a result of customer satisfaction. This satisfaction is largely influenced by the customer's perception of good value, which is created by satisfied, loyal and productive employees. Such a workforce is a result of internal quality embracing workplace and job design, providing the right tools for the job, careful employee selection and development, rewards and recognition.

Service capability pyramid

The service profit chain spotlights the need to create service capability – the tools and equipment combined with the people, skills and leadership to deliver great service. This can be portrayed as a pyramid, as shown in Figure 2.3. The base of the pyramid (level 1) is the platform of good workplace design. Attractive working conditions permit the recruitment of the right calibre of people (level 2). Service staff need a carefully designed induction and ongoing training to perform to a high standard (level 3).

Working harmoniously and decisively as an empowered team is the next step (level 4). The pinnacle (level 5) comes from leaders who personify service leadership.

Level 5	Leadership role models
Level 4	Empowered teams
Level 3	Skills: Induction and training
Level 2	People: Picking brand ambassadors
Level 1	Workplace: Designed to succeed

FIGURE 2.3 Service capability pyramid

Level 1: Workplace designed to succeed

The workplace design has a practical and an emotional impact on the staff serving the customer and the back-office staff supporting the front-line staff. The height, reach and comfort of chairs make a significant difference to the performance of ticket office staff, sitting serving customers for an 8-hour shift. Telephone headsets need to be ergonomic and effective for call-centre operators. The right tools for the job make a powerful impact on results. Shaw and Ivens (2002) tell of the laptop technology supporting sales of gas and electric fireplace installation services at Centrica. Salespeople can illustrate designs of gas or electric fires with surrounds. They can take digital photos of a customer's lounge and superimpose different designs on the fireplace until the customer is happy. Quotes can be given to customers on the spot. The new technology raised conversion rates from 35% to 43% in 18 months.

Beyond the practical aspect, there is an emotional dimension. Charlie Trotter's Chicago restaurant was named the best in North America by *Wine Spectator*. Journalist Ed Lawler (2001) describes the infrastructure behind the scenes as 'the best that money can buy'. He adds, 'In the kitchen are custom-made French Bonnet stoves with solid brass hinges, pieces of artwork to make the environment more pleasant and smoke-eating vents built into the stainless ceiling that purify the air and remove the grime.' Trotter says, 'People know that they are going to have the best things to work with here ... they have a boss who cares enough to buy the best so they can work at the top of their game.'

There may be other business objectives that shape the choice of infrastructure. When British Airways moved its headquarters to Waterside in 1998, the design concept by architect Niels Torp featured six horseshoe-shaped buildings backing on to an internal 'street'. This street is the social hub of the building, through which all staff exit and enter. This encourages chance encounters between staff from different departments. Most of the offices are open plan – again to facilitate collaboration. The high level of natural light supports a pleasant environment and allows people to see and recognise each other from a distance.

First Direct, the UK telephone bank, makes it easy for employees to focus on work by removing some of the associated hassles of life. For example, there is a concierge at the Leeds office building. She is quick to reassure you that she works for a bank not a hotel. She adds that, 'Because everyone is on site most of the day they don't get a chance to do things like go to the post office or pick up prescriptions. We do shoe heeling, dry cleaning, any sort of ad hoc requests, depending on limitations of course. Everyone's friendly – you're doing a job for somebody so everyone really appreciates what you do for them.'

Level 2: Picking brand ambassadors

Recruiting and selecting the right type of people is another key dimension. When each employee is seen as a brand ambassador, it is essential that recruitment be handled with great care. This means that specific ideal characteristics are sought and developed. It is significant that organisations recognised as great service providers rarely recruit staff from rivals in the same industry.

> organisations recognised as great service providers rarely recruit staff from rivals in the same industry

Personality characteristics are more important than existing technical skills. First Direct makes a practice of recruiting staff with appropriate attitudes from outside the financial services industry:

> *Do I look for someone with previous banking experience? No! Do I look for people who have got very high keyboard skills? No! Do I look for someone with personality, energy, passion and attitude? Yes!*
>
> David Mead, Chief Operating Officer, First Direct, quoted by Shaw and Ivens, 2002

Southwest Airlines, the US-based originator of no-frills flying, finds its staff from anywhere but its airline competitors. It looks for staff with empathy, and its selection process involves group activities culminating in each potential employee making a speech about why they should be recruited. The 'People Department' team watch the other candidates for demonstrations of empathetic behaviour rather than listening to the specific presentations. Who is nodding, smiling and encouraging? These are the kind of people who will make passengers genuinely welcome on board or on the phone. The candidate polishing his notes for his presentation while another speaks is unlikely to be a supportive colleague.

A brand value of international delivery firm UPS is speed. Reportedly (and perhaps tongue in cheek), the company heroes are those who can make a delivery to a building while their van is at a red stop light, returning before the lights change to green. You can imagine that a candidate trudging slowly into an interview would depress their chances of employment! A senior executive at TSB Bank used to leave a scrumpled ball of paper on the floor of the interview room when recruiting bank branch staff. He would watch to see which candidates naturally reached to place it in the waste bin. It was one of a series of indicators to suggest that a person might have the right attributes and standards to succeed in the role. For Charlie Trotter, the behaviour at the end of an interview can be illuminating. Does the candidate push their chair back under the table after rising, do they help clear cups, glasses or napkins from the table? Southwest Airlines has rejected an application from a brilliant pilot who was rude to a receptionist.

Eurostar, the London to Paris train operator, supplements interviews with tests for personality rather than technical competence. One of these tests is to send candidates out on the station concourse with instructions to engage three customers in conversation. If they cannot do this, they are patently unsuitable to be a member of the customer services team.

A number of retailers including Miss Selfridge and Prêt a Manger will ask good interview candidates to work a trial shift, so that they can be observed in action. Holiday Inns 'audition' potential food and beverage staff. This enables the peer group to express views on the new person's suitability as a team member. Of course, a side benefit of recruiting the right-minded people is that it ensures a flow of suitable people for senior roles. According to Prêt a Manger, 60% of its shop managers began as team members.

Firms must recruit staff who live the brand values in their behaviour. These people have the capability and natural flair to work in the manner of the service value proposition. For example, Enterprise Rent-A-Car has a strongly competitive company culture. Unique in the hire car business it focuses recruitment on graduates. And within the graduate category Enterprise has its eye on a particular type of person. Irrespective of the university or grade, their focus is on attracting the right people for the business: entrepreneurial, focused, success-orientated and sociable. University time spent socialising or playing competitive sport can create the characteristics of employees who will succeed at Enterprise. Their website **www.erac.com** says:

> *Hang out with Enterprise people long enough and you'll notice that, despite their personable nature, most seem to have the competitive fire of a great athlete or business tycoon.*

> *It's all about high fives, beating the competition and pushing ourselves.*

In keeping with their competitive culture, Enterprise Rent-A-Car have won awards recognising them as a better employer, from

Business Week (USA), *Report on Business* (Canada), *The Times* (UK), *Irish Independent* (Eire) and *Fair Company* (Germany). Brands must practice what they preach says loyalty expert Frederick Reichheld, who recommends careful recruitment as one of the key principles for creating long-term customer relationships.

Level 3: Skills to hit the ground running

Induction is the critical bridge between recruitment and successful employment. Great service providers need a world-class induction process. Carphone Warehouse, for example, insist that new starters cannot serve or even greet a customer until they have completed two weeks of intensive training and passed a strict assessment exercise.

Twenty-point checklist

Here is my checklist to evaluate your induction programme for new starters:

1. **Written offer** Does the formal offer of employment include an outline of the induction programme?

2. **Buddy** Is the new starter given a buddy from their future peer group?

3. **Early contact** Does the buddy make contact before the start date?

4. **Pre-start information** Does the new starter receive full details of start date, time, and place and to whom they should report?

5. **Looking forward to meeting you** Is contact made a couple of days before starting?

6. **Welcome** Do Human Resources, line manager and senior executive all welcome the new starter?

7. **Health and safety** Are health and safety issues covered on the first day?

8. **Work location** Is this ready and equipped for the new starter?

9. **Peer group introductions** Is there a programme of introductions to colleagues?

10. **Department relationships** Is there a programme of introductions to related departments and support services?

11 **Vision and values** Are company vision and values described to the new starter? And how are they demonstrated in practice?

12 **History and structure** Is the new starter made aware of company history and structure, and connections with sister companies?

13 **Customers and competitors** Is the new starter briefed on the needs, expectations and characteristics of customers (external or internal)? Can they observe, meet or visit customers? Are they briefed on how a customer should feel after a service encounter? Do they know names of the competitors and what their strategies are?

14 **Products and services** Is the new starter able to see, feel or experience the products or services provided? Are they shown the customer benefits and competitive advantages?

15 **Procedures and practices** Is the new starter briefed and able to carry out procedures and practices related to their role?

16 **Specific skills training** Is there an audit of skill needs and access to suitable training programmes, specific early job experiences and related projects?

17 **Continuous professional development** Is the new starter encouraged to develop themself?

18 **Review process** Is the progress of the new starter reviewed regularly – end of day one, end of week one, end of week two, end of first month, end of first quarter? Does the review include their line manager and a buddy?

19 **Sign off** Is there a formal point when they are recognised as full team members?

20 **Support to new starters** At the end of the induction programme, is the 'signed off' employee encouraged to act as a buddy to a future new starter?

Ritz-Carlton offers best practice in training for its upscale hotels around the world. The company sees induction as a vital moment for new recruits. They have some interesting induction practices. For example, on day 1 new recruits in the training room are ordered to say 'No' loudly and repeat it at a higher volume. Then they are instructed that this was the last time they will say 'no' in the hotel.

Ritz-Carlton aims to respond *positively* to every guest. The response may be in another form from the request, or cost a little more, or take longer, but you cannot make a guest feel good by saying 'no'. For more insight into how induction training and early job experiences are handled by Ritz-Carlton see 'My week as a room service waiter at the Ritz' by Paul Hemp (2002). Ritz-Carlton has a Learning Institute that offers employee-training seminars to other industries.

Training and development

Training and ongoing development maintain the momentum (see Figure 2.4). Training obviously includes upgrading technical skills and responding to market changes. Examples are improved patient admission procedures in a hospital, diagnostic procedures for new models in the motor industry or continual professional development in a consultancy. New legislation may require staff training to ensure comprehension and compliance, for instance financial institutions must make staff aware of changes to laws in checks for money laundering.

FIGURE 2.4 Training and development

Secondly, training and development supports the introduction of new procedures designed to save money or time in order to give better value to customers. A faster checkout system in a hotel is an example here.

Thirdly, training such as role playing the handling of difficult customers or language skills can increase staff confidence. Cross-training to give staff an understanding of the skills needed by other departments can improve their confidence in the whole organisation. Many customers have an instinct for detecting servers who are nervous or unprepared and they avoid them to seek service staff with an air of self-assuredness. Training and role play can guide staff to finish the service encounter on a high note.

feeling valued is a key contributor to staff retention

Fourthly, and in the longer term, investing time and money in training programmes, mentoring schemes and development exercises shows the employee that they are valued. Feeling valued is a key contributor to staff retention. Carphone Warehouse invest four times the average amount per head on training compared with other UK retailers. The firm benefits through having lower staff turnover in a sector bedevilled by staff moving on quickly.

However, there is a danger.

Any of these training interventions could change the experience of the customer. Checks for money laundering could meet legal requirements but feel offputting to new investors. Automated systems may deliver time improvements at the expense of the customer relationship. It is essential that the core of every training initiative be based on the value proposition.

Remind and focus on the priorities of the value proposition:

- Which are the key customer groups and how is this training relevant to them?
- What benefits are we offering and how does the training underwrite them?
- What is our price level and how does the training justify this?
- What is our distinctive way of meeting customer needs and how is this maintained or refined?

Training ensures that your people meet standards in performing the technicalities of the service. But it must also reinforce the offer and especially the 'way in which we serve customers', the distinctive feeling that contact with your brand evokes.

Level 4: The empowered team

Empowerment is a key part of the platform for success of Nordic Bank Handelsbanken, acclaimed Bank of the Year 2009 for the 19th year running, by a jury of *Privata Affärer*, a Swedish periodical for private finances. Handelsbanken – with over 700 branches worldwide – does not have sales targets or bonus schemes, but instead has a long-established culture of empowered teams who focus on customer satisfaction.

Team commitment is essential. One employee can ruin the service experience for the customer. He might fail to carry out the task correctly. She might criticise a fellow employee. He might blame another department for a shortfall. She might project the wrong image, dress standards or behavioural expectations. Yet when the service goes well, it is almost always the result of a team effort. The customer may take the whole operation for granted or even credit the front-liner who finishes well, but behind the scenes an entire team was involved in delivering the correct service experience. To keep this in the mind of all employees, everyone at Amazon (even CEO, Jeff Bezos) must spend two days every two years on the customer phones just to get a feel for the customer. It is the co-ordinated effort of the whole team that fashions a positive customer experience. Thus in a complex service environment like a hospital, a consultancy, an airline or a retail business, creating and sustaining teamwork is a vital attribute for success.

Nine-point checklist for effective teamwork

There are many approaches and answers to bringing about effective teamwork. From my service experience, the following checklist will help to deliver the highest impact on results:

1. **Customer-focused teams** Organise teams by the customer groups served rather than by function. Alternatively, create a matrix reporting system.

2. **Self-selecting teams** Allow teams to have a say in assessing and accepting potential new team members. Sandwich retailer Prêt a Manger does this.

3 **Limit the team size to a maximum of 12 to 15 players** More than 15 players and the sense of belonging diminishes.

4 **Create opportunities to meet and bond** Familiarity with colleagues leads to favourability. First Direct encourages car sharing and provides an on-site Costa Coffee venue for staff to socialise, with snooker and table-football areas for more active employees.

5 **Allow teams to influence work design** Establish formal suggestion schemes and informal work process improvement discussions and ensure that action follows.

6 **Involve teams in designing and updating the working environment**.

7 **Set team goals** Budget resources to enable the achievement of team goals.

8 **Competitive atmosphere** Introduce elements of competition with other teams, enough to stimulate loyalty, but not so much it constrains inter-team collaboration.

9 **Provide team recognition and rewards**.

The value proposition will identify which customer groups you are serving and the benefits you are offering. Where standardisation, absolute consistency and cost control are essential a 'production line' approach is correct. Similarly, where safety and legal controls are strict, there is one right way of doing things. Airline security staff screening passengers for weapons and explosives rightly have a procedure to follow.

> empowered employees are able to use their judgement to finish on a high note

Where the value proposition calls for speedy responsiveness to customer circumstances, then a degree of empowerment is needed. Empowerment in a service context means giving employees the desire, skills, tools and authority to serve the customer differentially according to their judgement of the needs of the situation. Empowerment tends to require better calibre employees who may command higher wages. Empowered employees are able to use their judgement to finish on a high note. On the downside, it results in less consistent service. However, empowerment normally increases job satisfaction for employees and increases ratings for flexibility and responsiveness from customers. It often generates positive word-of-mouth recommendation from delighted customers.

Empowerment is not abandonment. It requires four conditions to work successfully:

- **Desire** Selecting employees who enjoy interacting with customers and using their judgement.
- **Skills** Providing experience, peer group contact and training so that these employees develop the ability to form good judgements.
- **Tools** Giving access to guidelines and relevant information such as cost of recovery options, customer lifetime value, decision tools and review processes to support quality decision-making.
- **Authority** Delegating authority to operate and make decisions within certain financial or risk limits.

Successful empowerment is a continuous feedback process reviewing situations and decisions and refining best practices. The intent is that the firm responds quickly and correctly to individual customer requests and learns from each new situation. Charlie Trotter (see Lawler, 2001) has strict guidelines for service standards, but 'there is enormous latitude for an infectious spontaneity, flexibility and commonsense resourcefulness on the part of the service team'. He may ask later why servers have given away a bottle of wine, but there is absolutely no requirement to justify beforehand. The server is on the floor dealing with the guests and an immediate decision is appropriate. Trotter's message to his people is 'I completely trust you. Do it. I am sure you have your reasons.'

Different service organisations choose appropriate levels of empowerment.

Level 5: Leadership role models

Service employees observe and copy the actions of top management far more attentively than they listen to their words. The behaviours of senior executives are significant. Have agents seen top management spend time listening in on the telephones in the call centre? Do senior executives ever serve customers themselves? Do they visit, meet and listen to customers? Do they adopt key customers? Do they seek out lost customers to learn where things have gone wrong? Do they champion new service methods? Do they listen to internal suggestions of better ways to serve customers? Are they familiar with current customer feedback? Do they recognise staff going the extra mile for customers? Do they tell stories of excelling in serving customers? Do they personify the brand values in their contact with company people and customers? It is 'do as I do' not 'do as I say'.

Best practice in employee communications is surprising. A lesson from Colin Mitchell's article 'Selling the brand inside' is that organisations may inundate employees with briefings (Mitchell, 2002). Email has made it easy to overload people with repetitive communications. People soon learn to ignore over-communication. Less is more. Mitchell's research recommends that you must choose your moment. A turning point such as a new strategy, a company merger or takeover, the appointment of a new senior executive or an external crisis will link interest and a readiness to listen. He also recommends that internal brand messages be handled using the skills of marketing communications.

If the aim is to encourage employees to outperform competitors, then the maxim 'show not tell' can be used creatively. Charlie Trotter encourages staff to eat out at other restaurants to understand and report back on how it feels from the customer's side. Experiencing a competitor's service can raise the game or focus attention on the key differentiators that truly impact on customer perceptions.

Long-term retention, long-term success

People are the platform for the service brand. The basis for service delivery commences with creating the conditions whereby employees (and contractors) are best able and motivated to deliver service quality. In 'Breaking the cycle of failure in services', Schlesinger and Heskett (1991) identified the critical nature of employee retention to create capability to deliver excellent service. Some years ago I learnt that Marriott International had made an award for excellence to the Swansea Marriott Hotel. Shortly afterwards, I visited this hotel. The general manager modestly placed the credit for this accolade on the knowledge and skills of the 'associates' (as Marriott terms employees), and commented that her staff turnover was 19% per year. Contrast this with the 100–120% turnover found in rival hotels. This is the true explanation for the excellence of her hotel service.

Measure and compare operational management on staff turnover. Improvement will follow and management will naturally find creative ways of enhancing internal quality.

You create the platform for success through the right service value proposition, the right internal service quality and the right people, trained and motivated. From this service capability pyramid, you can design the eight acts to deliver a positive experience so customers return and recommend and the service profit chain delivers its profit.

part 2

Acts

Managing expectations – preconceptions

Act 1 sets the scene.

Good service exists in the customer's mind. So how do you win new prospects who will continue buying as loyal customers? The answer is to shape initial expectations so that the lasting perception is positive. If the prologue to the play over-sells the drama, theatre patrons will be disappointed. Therefore, expectation management begins before the service has started. In this chapter I look at three ways in which preconceptions arise and how they can be influenced or managed. Finally, I consider three different categories of service business, applying the principles of expectation management to each one in turn. Preconceptions are the first area of focus in shaping the service performance on the satisfaction curve, as in Figure A1.1.

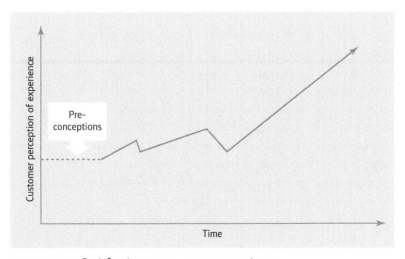

FIGURE A1.1 Satisfaction curve – preconceptions

Discovering about you

New services appear. From Garlik – a hard-nosed protection scheme against identity theft – to an imaginative luxury indulgence like Panties by Post. All the time, new providers enter existing markets. There is a constant flux. So how does the buyer learn about new services and new providers? How can you reach potential customers?

There are three ways that buyers can become aware of your service offerings:

1 **Direct communications (advertising/promotional messages)** These are explicit promotional communications designed to build awareness among target prospects, leading to interest, hopefully desire and ultimately purchase and repurchase. In addition there are implicit messages, signalled through cues and associations, that draw prospects to form their own expectations of the service you would provide.

2 **Media relations (the PR perspective)** These are the reports, views and recommendations published by the media, rightly or wrongly adjudged by prospects to be an independent viewpoint.

3 **Word-of-mouth recommendation (referral)** These are the reports of existing customers or users who give feedback from their experiences, which may be in the form of a direct conversation or a more distant communication like an individual comment on TripAdvisor or a personal blog.

Potential customers place greater value on the verdict of the media and even higher worth on the opinions of other users. In developed markets, prospects are often cynical about the veracity of advertising and direct communication directly from a business with an interest in selling to them. They may take greater note of the signs and cues revealed by non-verbal communications. You might term this the organisational body language. In sum, they combine all the sources in a form of triangulation, which synthesises all the viewpoints (see Figure A1.2).

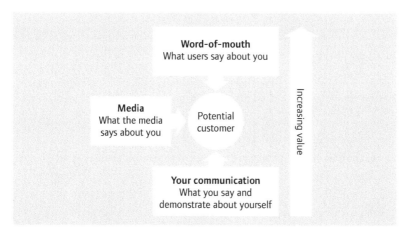

FIGURE A1.2 Sources of pre-information

The Goldilocks proposition

Our objective is to influence or manage preconceptions that achieve two purposes:

▌ Make the firm or business appear attractive to the target prospect

▌ Influence preconceptions so that it will be possible to delight the customer with a strong ending

This requires that we do not under-promise and in so doing fail to win the business of the prospect. It also requires that we do not over-promise and subsequently disappoint the customer with service below expectation. This is sometimes called a 'Goldilocks' proposition after the fairy story where the little girl found the first bowl of porridge too hot and the second too cold. The third bowl of porridge was 'just right'. It is this crucial balance that must be struck.

Best practices in expectation management

1 Direct communications

Let us focus first on the most controllable aspect, the direct communications from the service provider. These come in two forms:

1. Advertising/promotional messages including brochures, letters, website content, directory entries and paid-for adverts in media such as TV, radio and the press.

2. Implicit brand communications including indirect signals, visual indications and triggers for brand association.

Best practices for advertising/promotional messages

Be true-to-life Show photographs and images of genuine staff (not actors) serving real customers in a true environment. You can support credibility by giving their first names or the location where they work. Use quotations from customers to convey the actuality of the experience. Sleep Country is Canada's leading mattress retailer. The company's advertisements feature testimonials by satisfied customers. They're talking about the service, not the product. They say things such as, 'They came to deliver my mattress just when they said they would'. And 'I was so impressed when I saw the men putting on those little booties before they walked into my house'.

Use language, phrases and expressions used by regular customers. The airline easyJet has gone beyond this. The LWT 'fly on the wall' documentary series *Airline* shown on ITV is based around the passengers and staff at easyJet. In 2003 it was ITV's most popular factual programme. It shows passengers and staff on journeys, filming wedding proposals, business trips and once-in-a-lifetime experiences. Alongside entertainment, the programme aims to educate passengers about travelling with easyJet, showing the reality of late check-ins, incorrect travel documentation and the attempted carriage of prohibited items.

> promise what will be received. Avoid hype and puffery

Be accurate Promise what will be received. Avoid hype and puffery. Illustrate the benefits of the value proposition truthfully, as it happens in practice, not as an adman's ideal. The 2005 report of the Advertising Standards Authority (ASA) describes how 1500 UK travel agents were asked to state in their advertisements if availability of advertised offers is extremely limited. In April 2008, the National Health Service (NHS) launched a Code of Practice for Promotion of NHS Services, following the lifting of the ban on NHS advertising by the UK Department of Health. Setting realistic expectations of value or experience works to prevent later disappointment.

Test in-house first Advertising testing normally includes a 'beta test' to check the reactions of a representative sample audience. Best practice is to run an 'alpha test' before this, showing advertising concepts and scripts to front-line service staff. Use their feedback to refine and improve messages, visual devices and service promises.

Make a guarantee Give commitments and specific promises of what will be delivered. Ensure that serving staff (and the support teams behind them) understand the guarantees. Some service providers choose to back guarantees with poor performance payments. The Otter Tail Power Company, which is based in Minnesota and also serves North and South Dakota, was the highest rated utility company in the 2005 American Customer Satisfaction Index survey. Otter Tail commits to connection dates or compensates customers with $50. If a residential customer bill is inaccurate, in addition to correcting it, Otter Tail promises to credit the account with $25 ($150 for commercial customers). Monetary payments are not essential, but they will encourage customers to report failures and provide an easy tally of company performance.

Focus on benefits rather than price A low price depresses expectations of quality or consistency in service and may discourage service-orientated potential customers. Focusing on low prices may create the preconception that cost is more important than service standards. To counter this, Prestige and Performance Cars, a sports car specialist from Uxbridge, UK, draw attention to the benefits by offering buyers of used Porsches a choice of prices. You can buy 'as seen' with no warranty or guarantee or alternatively at 'full retail', which means that they send the car to an independent specialist for all necessary servicing and mechanical work to be carried out. You get a copy of the bills and a note of anything that will need attention in the future plus a

3000-mile warranty. For all these reasons it is preferable to place emphasis on the benefits to the customer, rather than the price.

Best practices for implicit brand communications

Show not tell Provide evidence, demonstration. It is better to illustrate speed, efficiency and accuracy than to talk about them. You would not believe a comedian who told you he was extremely funny; you need to hear a joke. A picture of smiling staff is more credible than a description. An example of innovation is better than saying you are innovative. Accenture is a global management consulting firm which focuses on its innovation. The Accenture website in 2007 featured an example of an innovative upgrade to the financial system of the National Aeronautic and Space Administration (NASA), highlighting an enhanced ability to streamline the agency's funds distribution and better overall funds control.

Use cues with psychological connections If the carriages are clean, the customer expects the train service to be punctual. If the lorries are washed and well maintained, the customer thinks the contents will be wholesome. Well-lit premises imply bright behaviours. Legible signs imply accessibility. Simple straightforward wording in a brochure suggests a transparent approach, whereas extensive small print conditions at the foot of a letter could be detrimental in conveying trustworthiness.

Align all the aspects Potential customers may read several different advertisements and then search the company's website before making an exploratory phone call. It is therefore important that the messages, vocabulary and tone of voice of adverts, website and phone teams are consistent. Customers notice and distrust inconsistency. For instance, intrusive communications for a discreet personal service may be counter-productive.

Consider colour associations These are powerful subliminal cues to convey virtues and capabilities. Note that they are culturally anchored, so that orange is seen as cheap and cheerful in the UK and the colour of royalty in the Netherlands. Red can imply urgency, passion, activity and speed. Blue can suggest calmness, reflection and professionalism. Green is often associated with environmental consideration.

2 Media relations

The second angle of the triangulation process is the media perspective where the tool of influence (beyond providing good service) is through public relations (PR). The media is a tough constituency because its audience pays more attention to bad news than good. Hence the best practices are often based around avoidance of problems, leaving the positive story to shine out.

Best practices for media relations

Respond speedily to the media Making it easy to confirm a story or providing a quote or factual information rapidly and accurately. Many service businesses have a section of their website for media offering facts, figures, contacts and downloadable images.

Be a good neighbour Being a considerate neighbour in the community can lead media and prospects to form a positive preconception of a business. For example, Charlie Trotter's staff sweep and hose down the pavement of West Armitage Avenue in front of the restaurant every day, removing litter from several blocks around, making it a better environment for guests and neighbours alike.

Be a good citizen Public awareness and concern about global warming, waste and environmental impact has increased significantly in recent years. Media attention is increasing. Service businesses must act as good global citizens, reviewing their behaviours and the impact of their actions to ensure that they are moving in the right direction. The UK do-it-yourself retailer B&Q regularly donates waste materials such as timber and paint to community projects.

Present a positive view Any negativity may result in a shadow on the service brand itself. Therefore a positive focus on building the industry standards and reputation is appropriate. Players in the rapidly growing self-storage industry compete strongly for custom yet collaborate in their trade body – the Self Storage Association – to develop better industry standards for users in the future. Positive businesses do not knock rivals, they out-score them with relevant benefits for customers.

3 Word-of-mouth recommendation

> for service businesses recommendations are vital

The third angle is the perspective of existing customers and what they say about you. Word-of-mouth recommendations are important for all businesses. For service businesses recommendations are vital because the actions performed are intangible, variable and hard for potential buyers to compare rationally beforehand. So what are the best practices in generating positive word-of-mouth endorsement?

Best practices for word-of-mouth recommendation

Give consistently considerate service Believe that customers are rational beings who will recognise and recommend considerate service experiences. Nordic bank Handelsbanken specialises in providing highly personalised banking services to individuals and corporates. Operations are not centralised and decision lines are remarkably short. As an example, a customer of SHB (Handelsbanken) was traversing Sweden to attend a wedding, and hundreds of kilometres from home realised their wallet had been left behind. Life is a challenge with no cash, cards or identity, so in desperation the customer walked into a branch of SHB in the middle of Sweden. The teller explained that with no identification, you cannot draw money from your bank account, but at Handelsbanken, we trust people ... so let me lend you some money from my own account and repay me when you return home!

Identify what matters to customers The toilet paper brand Charmin knows that consumers rarely talk about toilet paper. However, people often talk about the availability and cleanliness of public toilets. With this insight, Charmin sponsors an iPhone application to help consumers find clean public toilets worldwide. The information – from information website **www.sitorsquat.com** – covers 78,000 toilets worldwide and includes opening hours, facilities such as baby changing tables and a consumer rating facility.

Something for the loved ones Many conversations feature partners or friends, parents, grandparents or children. Special consideration for someone close to the customer can result in positive word-of-mouth communication. Award-winning tailor-made travel company Trailfinders had booked a family of four to go on holiday to Mauritius. And then the call came to say that the new Harry Potter book was about to be released and the children wanted first-day copies. The parents saw no alternative but to cancel their holiday! Rather than let this happen, Trailfinders located a bookshop in Mauritius for them, checked they would be stocking the book and asked them to reserve a copy. The parents were delighted. How many people were told this story?

Recover brilliantly from service errors Fixing a service problem convincingly often results in the customer feeling more positive and more inclined to recommend.

Give an explanation when service achieved has been 'lucky' Tell them when they have benefited from good luck in a particular service delivery, if this is unrepeatable, so that they will not expect the same every time.

Identify your champions Pareto's law tells us that, amongst all customers, there will be around 20% who give 80% of your recommendations. You may be able to identify these serial recommenders by asking new customers what brought them to you. There are also some characteristics of people who recommend frequently: they are 'early adopters' who take a special interest in new services, so that they are in a position to gain social status by highlighting them to their friends. They have very wide social connections. Malcolm Gladwell (2002) in *The Tipping Point* calls them 'mavens' and draws attention to their very extensive networks. Allegedly women recommend more frequently to more people than men – a delighted female customer will broadcast to 23 friends while the equivalent male just mentions it to his two best buddies!

When the Baltic Arts centre opened in Gateshead, UK, an early move was to offer previews to every taxi-driver and hairdresser in the district. The assumption was that both these professions had the opportunity and stimulus to talk to their customers. If they had visited the Arts Centre they could and would recommend it from a basis of knowledge.

Feed your champions Provide your recommenders with good material. In Andy Sernovitz's book, *How Smart Companies Get People Talking* (2006), he recommends finding the 'talkers' and then to give them 'topics' – something interesting to say about you. They need nuggets of information, news and recent developments, curious stories, memorable facts and figures. Think particularly of the items that will prove persuasive to potential new customers. Volvo cars have such recognisable advertisements that many non-Volvo drivers skip them. However, the faithful Volvo owner reads every word. Hence the copywriters place memorable facts and statistics under photographs and at the end of paragraphs where the owners will note them. Hopefully they will repeat them to the potential Volvo buyers who skipped the ads.

Seek feedback and refine You should seek feedback, researching what is said about your service. The information can be valuable to improve the product, update the service offer or to make changes to shape perceptions. Ideally you should join the conversation. An open forum, conference or customer event facilitates direct contact. In addition there are virtual opportunities with discussion areas on websites and blogs.

To summarise, the best form of expectation management is to view pre-purchase communication as an opportunity to give a taste or impression that is as genuine as possible. It should be positive in conveying the benefits that a new customer will find when they proceed.

Application to specific types of service

Each sector has its own unique characteristics. It is hard to apply every precept to all service businesses. Beyond a certain level, generalisations carry risks. It is possible, however, to classify service sectors.

There are a number of dimensions that distinguish the categories of service. The most critical is the volume of business. High volume businesses tend to have low levels of customisation and moderate degrees of customer contact. Equipment and systems are crucial. Employee discretion is restricted. This type of service business is known as *mass service*. A second category of service businesses has lower volumes and moderate customer contact. Service can be more personal and customised with more employee discretion allowed. This type of business is known as a *service shop*. A third category of low volume, more expert services provide high levels of customer contact, personal and individual customisation with greater staff discretion. This type of business is known as *professional service*. See Table A1.1 for a summary of service typology (see also Silvestro *et al.* (1992)).

TABLE A1.1. Service typology

Service type	Characteristics	Examples
Mass service	High volume, low to moderate customer contact, standardised, less staff discretion	Airline, bank, hotel, retailing, train-operating company
Service shop	Moderate customer contact, more personal, customised, more staff discretion.	Hospital, travel agent, car repair
Professional service	Low volume, high contact, expert, personal, customised, significant staff discretion	Doctors, lawyers, accountants, architects

I will focus attention on specific requirements for these three categories of services in the application section at the end of each chapter.

HOW TO APPLY

Preconceptions: prospects and how to manage their expectations

APPLICATION: MASS SERVICE

Airlines, banks, hotels, logistics firms, retailing, train-operating companies

People Few people are involved in delivering these services and the interactions are a small but notable part of the experience. Employees are involved especially in the entry and exit stages. New customers should be able to recognise staff uniforms. Show uniformed staff in context on the website or pre-service literature. Where high levels of advice are expected, the training and ability of the staff will be a relevant virtue to include in advertising and communication.

What to expect Publicity must illustrate exactly what customers will see first time around. Show the setting for the check-in and hotel reception on the website for example. No surprises. You might give travellers or guests pre-information about questions they will be asked or procedures to follow. Give prior warning if personal identification is needed to open an account or to check-in. Advertising messages and external signing are important in conveying the brand impression. For example, the automotive brand BMW ensure that dealer premises have a design highlighting chrome and glass, conveying a feeling of engineered modernity.

Finding the location Websites need postcodes for satellite navigation systems and location maps showing how to find the hotel, railway station or airport. Test the print-size on 60-year-olds to ensure it is legible across the age range. Test colours under low-light circumstances – red on black has too little contrast to be read by a car interior light. Give guidance on public transport and likely time and cost allowances to be made. For complex facilities like large railway stations or airports, site plans or direction markers are useful. Aim for easy access first time around.

Queries and questions Place frequently asked questions (FAQs) in a visible way on the website and couch these in the conversational language that real customers speak. Update sites with feedback from new customers previously unfamiliar with the service. Staff responding to phone, letter and email enquiries should be alert for signs that the caller is a new customer. Because regular and repeat customers heavily use these services, it is easy to overlook and disappoint new users.

Check for mismatches Hotels typically have a number of spacious, airy, well-furnished rooms and these are the ones featured in website photographs. Yet in practice, price seekers buying online for web discounts find that they never see these rooms. Instead they are allocated attic rooms. The better rooms are reserved for those who pay standard rate. It is an appropriate value-based strategy. However, it is important that Internet buyers see the rooms that they will be allocated to ensure that their expectations are set correctly.

Word-of-mouth recommendation Retailers need to activate word-of-mouth endorsement by their existing customers and so retail theatre comes into play. These are special events designed to capture the interest of shoppers through information or entertainment. For example, DVD, games and music retailer HMV will book well-known bands to perform in their Oxford Street store. The aim is to stimulate customer conversations about HMV among music-lovers. Word-of-mouth is also important to web retailers and Internet banks who encourage customers to recommend others. Member-get-member and reward strategies are in place to show appreciation of recommenders. The bank First Direct has grown through recommendation and bases much of its promotional strategy on the satisfaction of current customers.

▶

Specific banking issues Banks have a particular challenge in setting preconceptions because customers hold strong perceptions that all banks are identical. The industry stresses solidity and banks tend to move in step. The advertising strategies seem similar, being product-focused and using common phrases and generic illustrations. The lesson of commodity marketing is that being close to the customer and responding with better service achieves advantage. Rather than sounding the same as other banks, a bank should find its own distinctive style of behaviour, as described in the previous chapter.

Hospitals, car repairers, travel agents

People Although there are relatively few staff per customer involved in the service, staff have an important role in reassurance. Therefore some information about staff selection, qualifications, experience, training and skills is important for new customers. The tailor-made travel company Trailfinders encourage their consultants to describe their own travel experiences to customers. They invite customers to speak to someone who has been – between them their consultants have travelled in over 96% of the world's countries. This gives them strong credibility as advisers.

What to expect With a high degree of customisation occurring, the customer/patient will be concerned that they will be treated individually. Expectations should be set in case their preconceptions exceed what can actually be delivered. For example, individuality can mean time variability, which may result in waiting time or delays. Unanticipated queues can cause disappointment. Where specific information (medical or vehicle documentation for instance) must be brought to an appointment, it is important that this is spelt out in instructions and included in any summary of information.

How to find the location If there is any difficulty for a first-time patient or customer finding the location, clear guidance in the form of satnav directions, landmarks, address and a map should be provided in external communications. This is often an issue for hospitals where urgent first-time visits are likely to involve levels of stress. Smith and Wheeler (2002) cite University Hospital, in Augusta Georgia, who placed additional road signs further out in all directions from the campus. 'Hospital 3 miles' created reassurance, especially for newcomers to the area. Good signing, good directions (again legible by eyes of all ages), clear instructions for public transport. Many UK hospitals have very limited areas for car parking and charges may be greater than occasional visitors expect. Therefore include information on the best places to park, coins needed, directions to parking, time to allow, busy periods and alternative travel methods. Not being able to park can cause additional tension.

Specific hospital issues For good preconceptions, staff policies should bar the wearing of nurses' uniforms on public transport for reasons of hygiene perceptions. Patients want hospitals to be beacons of good cleanliness practices.

Internal signing is another issue. Large hospitals are confusing buildings. Many of the department names seem similar to dyslexics and people whose first language is not English. This applies to patients, carers and hospital visitors. Clear signing should feature symbols, colour coding and help points. Every appointment letter should have a location map on the reverse or attached to it.

APPLICATION: PROFESSIONAL SERVICE

Accountants, architects, consultants, doctors, lawyers

Brand communication Many professional service businesses do not advertise either by convention or by internal rule. For example, management consulting firm McKinsey & Company eschews advertising. For prospective clients, perceptions of professional service firms are formed through word-of-mouth recommendation, media comment and reported actions, successes and failures. Name awareness can be supported through sponsorships and association with events such as seminars and conferences. For this reason

▶

typographical and image consistency is an important factor to avoid confusion with other firms in the same sector.

Results and consistent behaviour Doctors, lawyers, accountants and consultants face the challenge that most of the tasks they perform are unique in terms of the client and the circumstances. The right outcome is vital and success is obviously sought. Case histories illustrate successes by sector. However, with changing clients and new challenges, success is never guaranteed. Therefore the style and feeling evoked are also vital. Even if the result was not exactly as planned, the way the service was performed can be praised and promoted by the client to prospective clients. It is therefore crucial to have a house style of behaviour with a shared understanding of 'the perceptions we want to leave with the client'.

Word-of-mouth It is important to help happy clients know what you want them to say about you. Many clients appreciate the positive results achieved but they need guidance on the virtues to stress to potential clients. Ensure they understand your promotable virtue.

Starting well – first impressions

Three short Gs and a long E flat, 'dit-dit-dit-daaah', provide that unique opening to Beethoven's 5th symphony. Beethoven's secretary, Schindler, claimed that the composer called this opening 'Fate knocking at the door'. Whether it's a true story or not, the four notes have captured the attention of listeners with a distinctive first impression. The listener wants more. Act 2 begins to engage the customer as they gain their first contact (see Figure A2.1).

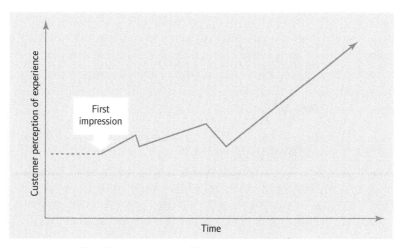

FIGURE A2.1 Satisfaction curve – first impressions

You only get one chance to make a strong first impression. J.M. Barrie began the story of *Peter Pan* with the intriguing words, 'All children, except one, grow up'. Similarly, Shakespeare invites interest with the brooding opening words of the play *Richard III*, 'Now is the winter of our discontent made glorious summer by this sun of York'.

The first impression is an invitation to take things further.

In service, David H. Maister offers two laws in his article 'The Psychology of Waiting Lines' (1985). His first law of service relates to the expectations and perceptions of the experience. Paraphrased, it says that if a customer receives better service than expected, he departs happy. The second law of service highlights the difficulty of recovering from a poor first impression, or as Maister puts it, 'It's hard to play catch-up ball'.

> in a retail store a perception will be gained in a minute

The first impression may be almost instantaneous as a website downloads – three seconds is more impressive than six. In a retail store a perception will be gained in a minute. Within professional services the initial impression may be generated in the first hour of contact. Typically we would see the first four minutes of any contact as a critical time when sensory perceptions are being absorbed. In their book, *Contact: The First Four Minutes*, Leonard and Natalie Zunic (1989), describe this phase as an audition. So how will you ensure that you pass the audition?

Like a successful audition

When an aspiring dancer enters for her audition, the panel sees her ballet shoes are new, they see the spring in her step, they hear her confident 'hello' and the first impression is completed by the expectation she sets with her explanation of the routine she will perform. Likewise, with your service audition, success comes from managing all four aspects of the first impression:

1. Tangible evidence.
2. Signals that create perceptions.
3. Greetings by staff.
4. Expectation setting.

Managing the tangible signs

Services are largely intangible. You cannot see insurance or consultancy. Service consistency cannot be judged until after the service has been performed, so customers subconsciously use tangible pieces of evidence to gauge the likely quality of the forthcoming service. Each tangible item plays a part in creating the overall impression. For example, a black stain on the white signboard of a dental practice could prejudice expectations of standards of the hygienist. There is no logical connection, but, in subliminal ways, the mind of the customer seeks cues on which to found their perceptions.

Step one is to identify all the tangible items that the customer may see. For this a fresh pair of eyes may be helpful. Ask a new member of staff, or an independent observer, to report on all the items that they came across in entering the premises (if this is a physical location). For phone services and websites, there are fewer cues.

At physical premises, the following list shows items that may arise on your checklist:

- Surroundings, neighbourhood.
- External signage.
- Maintenance standards of exterior of building, paintwork.
- Entrance portal, size, tidiness, cleanliness.
- Internal décor, lighting, up-to-date merchandising.
- Reception standards, furnishings, fittings, neatness, journals, promotional material, lighting, customer seating.
- Toilet facilities – design, cleanliness, accessibility.
- Employee dress/uniform design, colour, suitability and distinctiveness.
- Employee presentation – shoes, hair, tattoos, jewellery.

Documentation and paperwork are also important in creating initial impressions. A neatly written estimate conveys a professional stance. A clear layout, with legible print and obvious contact details can drive a positive customer opinion. Imagine a customer has received two estimates where the main attributes of work specification, timing and price are similar, then the choice criteria could come down to the easiest phone number to read. Trendy business cards with minimalist design, unique typeface and small print-size may suit the brand values of a design house selling to young urbanites, but would damage the prospects of more established organisations.

The aim is to look the part, to present an image and identity wholly consistent with the service value proposition. The Disney organisation wishes to portray a magical fairytale perception. Body piercings and tattoos on staff will contradict this impression (except perhaps for pirates!) and so Disney dress standards exclude these personal expressions. Consistency is essential. For example, if safety is an important aspect in the proposition, white lines making stair treads visible could be an important cue to support the right perception. These white lines will need repainting frequently in order always to appear pristine. Be aware that one single shortfall in standards of tangible items will be the factor that the customer notices.

> one single shortfall in standards of tangible items will be the factor that the customer notices

Signalling the right perceptions

First impressions are also created by less obvious cues. The mind assesses an environment through all the senses. Consider how each sense can contribute to the desired impression.

Sense of smell The nose detects aromas and the brain rapidly categorises them positively or negatively. Flowers in a reception area convey good feelings to most people. Even smokers dislike the smell of stale cigarette smoke – ever present by entrances where smoking is banned in offices. It is possible to engineer the right aromas. The scent of fresh bread wafting through a bakery is close to irresistible! English males have responded well to the light smell of newly mown grass piped through the air-conditioning of a retailer's gardening department – subliminally it may create a sense of context. However, the technique must be handled with care. A

Seattle grocery store used to spray the scent of strawberries in the entrance to its fruit and vegetable section, which led to increased sales and increased disappointment with the bland odourless berries when they were tasted.

Sense of hearing Background noise must be considered when setting the scene. The context is important. In some circumstances there is reassurance in the sound of bustle and laughter. It may convey that an establishment is well patronised and successful – an implied endorsement by existing customers. Background music may help the ambience of a clothing store.

For websites, sound is an optional extra in communicating with customers. It needs to be borne in mind that some customers cannot receive the sound, or choose to disable it when at work in an office for example. Furthermore the sound quality received will vary significantly. Selecting the right kind of music or the right voiceover is important. Both need to be in harmony with the service value proposition. Be wary of brand hijacking by the enthusiastic web designer.

Sense of vision Colour is important to create an atmosphere and ambience. The appropriate level of lighting can create feelings of calmness, harmony, energy and so on. Many of the visual aspects have been described above.

Sense of touch BMW has researched the perceptions created by different types of leather on steering wheels, different textures of metal for gearsticks and door handles. These are the limited surfaces that you touch in a car with bare skin. So the sensation caused is significant. What are the surfaces that your customers touch with bare hands? What impression might be created?

Sense of intuition A sense of confidence comes from signals like accurate presentation. Therefore accuracy of written details is an important judgement criterion for service businesses. Checking spelling is worth it. Systematically checking that customer names are written correctly is a sensible practice. Asking a customer how to spell an unusual name is always worthwhile: it achieves accuracy and also demonstrates that your company cares. Random checking of outgoing communications can be an appropriate way of identifying weak links.

Sense of time First impressions of the way customers' time is treated can be long lasting. Was the first appointment handled punctually? How is the waiting handled? The length of wait may be less important than the level of concern that is shown to customers in trying to provide service. Indifference to a new customer waiting for attention will damage the first impact. Recorded phone messages that say 'Your call is important to us' are counter-productive. Customers disregard what is said – it is actions that are taken seriously. Best practice says that the opportunity to leave a phone number for a callback service is better than a recorded apology. And when answered, the agent should acknowledge the length of wait and thank the new caller for their patience. Reassuring signs that every effort is directed to speeding the process will enhance the impression.

For websites the speed of downloading is a crucial factor. Is your site faster or slower than your direct competitors? Web patience is declining, so it may be worth forgoing sophistication for simplicity to achieve a higher speed. The website can also save customers time later, by preparing customers for the information they will need to provide at a later stage.

Showing that customers' time is valued is an important differentiator in many service businesses.

Greeting the new customer

The first personal contact for a customer at the start of a transaction is a memorable moment. Subsequently many of the interim communications will be forgotten in the passing of time. But the first contact may be recalled long after. It is therefore important that the interaction goes well and impressions are positive.

There are some business aspects to this greeting – confidence and professionalism. There are some personal aspects as well, such as warmth, friendliness and signals of respect. In most circumstances appropriate words of welcome will be extended with a mutual introduction. In a face-to face encounter, eye contact is important to show sincerity. In a phone greeting, this must be conveyed via intonation and expression. The best practice for opening phone calls is the formula shown in Figure A2.2.

> in a face-to-face encounter, eye contact is important to show sincerity

FIGURE A2.2 Best practice phone greeting

Remember that every individual has words and phrases that come easily to them. Some people want to begin with 'Hello' or 'Hi' and stumble over 'Good morning'. The richness of English vocabulary means there are probably a dozen acceptable opening greetings. Some individuals may choose to vary their opening. Others will stick to a standard phrase. The central issue is that a person sounds more at ease when they are using the words they feel more comfortable with. Provided brand standards are met, guidelines can be given, rather than strict instructions. The phrases 'My name is ...' and 'You are speaking to ...' have a specific benefit. The three or four words before the name highlight that an important piece of information is coming up that the customer may wish to note. When introductions begin with the name itself, most customers will fail to recall it.

Whether the initial contact is face-to-face, through web-chat or over the phone, it is important to achieve dialogue. This begins with understanding the need. It progresses to demonstrating listening through summarising and clarifying requests, orders or instructions. Normally it should end with agreement on any actions.

For the customer, you are the face and voice of the company. Anderson and Zemke (1998) recommend that in this situation the company representative should always use the pronoun 'I' rather than 'we'. The personal pronoun connotes personal ownership. The word 'we' adds some distance to the emotion and diminishes the degree of personal commitment. Never say 'they' to describe the company because this ruins the personal touch. It implies that you are unempowered and see the company as another party. Say 'I' not 'we' because to the customer you are the company. Furthermore the words 'company policy' detach the representative from the decision making. See Figure A2.3.

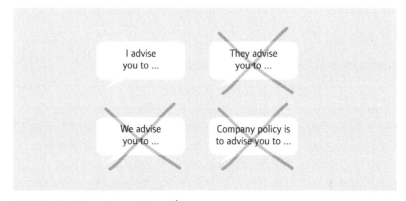

FIGURE A2.3 *I*, not *we*, never *they*

For consistency, the greeting should bring to life the adverb in your service value proposition. For example, a creative organisation might use an unusual and distinctive phase in their first greeting. A delivery organisation might speak more quickly than a legal practice.

Finally, the greeting must be honest in setting expectations of what the organisation will deliver and the style of working. An over-promise leads to disappointment later. Nor must it under-promise. Organisations that under-promise often lose the work to brands that better understand the way the world works.

Setting the right expectations

Expectations are being formed from the start. Explain to the customer what she will receive. Tell him what you cannot provide. Silence is always taken as consent. Anticipate and avoid potential misunderstandings. Indicate how you work. Outline what is a reasonable timescale. Define what 'good' looks like. Service researcher, Leonard Berry, proposes three steps to increase perceptions of service convenience (Berry *et al.*, 2002). He recommends:

1. Give information that reduces customers' uncertainties and anxieties about delays.

2. Help consumers to use the service properly.

3. Explain reasons for (potential) delays.

So how should the process of setting expectations be managed? My experience indicates some best practices.

An induction for customers

When a new employee joins the firm there is a clear procedure in place to induct them. This includes any safety information, introductions to people they will meet, what facilities are available, how to seek help, what the management expects in terms of performance and so on. New customers need an 'induction' too.

The induction will of course vary significantly between a complex interaction and a simple exchange. Here is a checklist to consider:

Customer induction – the six-point checklist

1. **Explain the role of the contact person and any other people they may meet** Honda car salespeople introduce new car buyers to the service manager who will handle vehicle servicing.

2. **Explain how to get in touch** This may mean providing a business card with contact details. Some financial services firms open accounts through branch staff and then show customers how to use Internet services for normal interactions thereafter. A management consultant might provide a back-up contact for times when they are away on engagements.

3 **Outline the facilities available and how best to access them** First Great Western shows rail customers how to use automatic vending machines to help them avoid peak time queues.

4 **Explain rules and procedures** Ryanair insists on all its passengers showing photo ID before they are allowed on the plane, even for domestic flights. Legendarily careful in spending money, Ryanair uses public relations to help train customers. For example, they might refuse to allow a celebrity to fly if they lack picture ID, and then leak the story to the newspapers. The subsequent coverage educates customers to follow their procedures. In a branded coffee shop, the first person takes the order and then hands the customer on to the barista who brews and pours the cup. Training customers to describe the size, flavour and preparation technique in the right sequence speeds service for everyone. Starbucks provide a guide to ordering coffee variants, which explains ordering protocol. In addition the firm has another technique to influence customers. When a customer places a specific order, the clerk repeats it for confirmation, but in the correct sequence. The clerk is not rebuking the customer, but rather training them for the next time. Some software houses invite new customers to join a user group.

5 **Capturing customer information** Often at the introductory stage the customer will be asked for information. For example, a claims history for an insurance quotation. It is important to set expectations of how many questions they face and how the information will be used to save them time in the future.

6 **Set time expectations** A phone agent promised to call a customer back with a decision 'shortly'. The customer waited by the phone for two hours and was angry when the call eventually came. The agent was puzzled because 'shortly' meant something different to him. The busy Hilton Hotel Barcelona well understands the time pressures of departing guests heading for the airport. As they check-in, guests are advised how long to allow for checkout, for a taxi to arrive and the journey to the airport.

Research new customers, after their first encounter, to check that your strategies are valid. Ask them what were their expectations? How were these formed? Use this to refine your expectation-setting process.

> service providers need to determine the genuine
> and realistic impression to convey to new
> customers

In conclusion, service providers need to determine the genuine
and realistic impression to convey to new customers. What will
customers receive and how will it be delivered? What must
we promise and deliver in order to succeed? Having decided
the correct expectation you must review all the means of
communicating this – spoken and signalled. Treat the first contact
as an audition with a dual objective: to win the customer's business
and to prevent future disappointment when you serve them.

HOW TO APPLY

First impressions: starting well

APPLICATION: MASS SERVICE

Airlines, banks, hotels, logistics firms, retailing, train-operating companies

Issues for retailers A retail experience provides the first
impression as the customer walks into the store. The pace of walking
on the street is faster than the normal speed of browsing in the shop.
Therefore the shop entrance is where the customer slows down.
According to retail expert Paco Underhill (2000), this area acts as a
'decompression zone'. The customer is adjusting to the atmosphere,
ambience, lighting, signs and merchandise. It is a lot to take in.

- Retailers need to simplify the complexity of the first few metres of
  walkway.

- Is the directional signing legible when the customer is walking at
  'pavement speed'?

- Many customers miss the rack of baskets at the doorway – do you
  need to place further racks further into the store? Customers with
  baskets are able to carry more and buy more.

▶

▌ Best practice retailing often involves encouraging the customer to walk around the whole store, so that they may see and buy impulse items. For example, when Ingvar Kamprad opened his new IKEA store in Stockholm in 1965, the layout was inspired by an earlier visit he had made to the New York Guggenheim museum. Here a single route took patrons past every work of art. Kamprad used the same concept of a single pathway through 45,800 square metres, enabling customers to see and buy from the entire range of merchandise. Have you identified the best way to direct customers around your store? Unless they know exactly where they are heading, most customers veer to the left as they enter. You can use this tendency to manage their pathway.

▌ Search convenience is one of the key discriminators of successful retailing identified by Seiders, Berry and Gresham (2000). Their research highlighted the positive perceptions of speed and ease that come when customers can find and select products quickly. They recommend integrating all the different enablers of focused merchandising, intelligent store design and layout and knowledgeable salespeople. Look at convenience from the customers' viewpoint.

Issues for banks For retail banking, the environment is also a driver of first impressions.

▌ Seeing immediately where to go for different types of service is important. For a banking website, is the navigation and speed of page opening competitive with other websites? In the branch, look at signs from the angle of a new and unfamiliar customer.

▌ Consider the ambience – more natural light makes a premise feel more accessible. Better lighting will make older customers feel more at ease.

▌ Consider the first words spoken. How does the teller greet the next face at the window?

Signs of safety and cleanliness Tangible signs are important for travel operations such as rail services, where the staff numbers are small compared with the volume of passengers, guests or customers. The tangible indicators will be the main source of first impressions.

▌ Safety is a consideration to some segments particularly in trains and planes where accidents receive long-lasting publicity. Therefore give close attention to indicators of good safety standards. For example, stairways should have high-visibility white lines regularly repainted on the step edges and/or non-slip edging. Platform edges should have well-maintained yellow safety lines. Seat pocket safety guides in planes should be smart, crisp and clean. Fire extinguishers in hotels should be dust-free.

▌ Passengers will not notice a clean plane or train. However, dirty carriages, poor external paintwork or dirty seats will sensitise them to look out for other potential problems. Poor quality finish in a hotel reception can lead to guests anticipating shortfalls elsewhere.

Greetings

▌ Greetings matter. In these businesses, because of large numbers of customers, there is limited personal contact. Therefore it is important to magnify the effect of every interaction. A smile, nod or cheery hello can carry its effect through the journey. Where passengers are categorised by service level, for example by business class and economy, the expectations of higher ticket prices is that there will be some personal service. The greeting is part of meeting this promise.

▌ First impression of customer care. You cannot give individual care to all customers through the journey – economic reality forbids this. However, by taking conspicuous care of elderly, inexperienced or disabled passengers, a clear message of caring is given to the remaining passengers. They witness the proactive support given to the needy. They gain the impression of care.

▌ Train operating companies in the UK employ revenue protection officers to check tickets on board. As the officer goes through the train, he can vary his opening comments, saying 'Hello' to the first person, 'May I see your ticket please', to the second, 'Good morning' to the third, then 'Tickets please'. And so on. The alternative is to repeat the same mantra to every passenger on the train, robbing passengers of any sense of individuality. Airlines have the same opportunity when checking seat belts prior to take-off.

▶

Setting expectations In these businesses, setting expectations must often be carried out through mass communication. Company websites are a valuable way for airlines and train operating companies to reach people before they travel. Checklists and advice can be given to new or infrequent travellers. Give guidance on time to allow through check-in. Provide special information to particular groups. For example, Southwest Airlines warns 'persons of size' that they will need to buy two tickets if they are too large to be able to sit between the armrests of a single seat.

Onboard signs indicating 'no mobile phones' set expectations of behaviour in quiet carriages. Giving out plastic bags marked 'Litter' can set expectations that travellers should place their cartons or uneaten food here for later collection.

APPLICATION: SERVICE SHOP

Hospitals, car repairers, travel agents

These businesses have high numbers of customers/patients, yet each is expecting a customised experience. They will include nervous first-timers. Therefore the right first impressions can allay the fears and doubts in the minds of these customers.

Tangible signs

▌ Hospitals are complex environments. Clear signing, site maps and often colour-coding of departments can help considerably. Symbols are important to communicate to people whose first language is not English or who may find reading departmental names confusing. At University Hospital, Augusta, Georgia, the sign 'Triage Station' meant nothing to emergency patients. Smith and Wheeler (2002) describe how it was re-named 'Care Point 1 – Reception'.

▌ Car repairers and automotive businesses need to give clear indications that a customer's vehicle is safe here. Positive signs are orderly parking bays, clean and unobstructed entrances, a brightly lit reception with up-to-date posters.

▌ Most travel agents fill their windows with price-based adverts and discount stickers. Yet Trailfinders believe that the magic of its destinations is more important. They sell the dream. Creating the first impression of adventure and delight is a more powerful message than simply 'we cut prices'.

Signalling perceptions For hospitals, cleanliness and catering are important because they reassure and are a way that users and carers can judge a hospital's standards – they create good or bad perceptions. Reception needs water fountains, toilets and vending machines to make it look patient-friendly.

For travel agents, perceptions of accuracy are crucial. Many travellers know the stories of denial of boarding when there is a single letter error in the spelling of the name on an airline ticket.

A challenge to hospitals (and other buildings where smoking is forbidden) is how to deal with the group of smokers standing outside the front door. Imagine the emotions of an asthma patient walking through the fug and smoke haze on their way to treatment. A solution is needed.

Greeting With hospitals in particular, staff should identify patients making their first visit to the hospital and give this group more support and information. Likewise, as service intervals for cars become greater, customer familiarity will be reduced. The welcome therefore assumes more significance.

APPLICATION: PROFESSIONAL SERVICE

Accountants, architects, consultants, doctors, lawyers

Professional services businesses differ from the mass service and service shops. With much higher personal involvement and an individually tailored proposition, the interaction is a fundamental part of the first impression.

▶

The impression comes from the people that new clients meet. How are they dressed? Can they show familiarity with the client's industry and company or create rapport with the individual client? How formal or welcoming are they? Do they personify the values of the firm?

The tangibles are also noticed by the new customer. Look at the standard of décor, the quality of the reception area and the meeting room environment from their perspective. What do written materials convey? Credibility may be damaged by out-of-date material on display. Showing examples of thought leadership in the literature racks can enhance profile.

Both the people and the tangibles must single-mindedly underline the positioning of the firm – the distinctive dimension chosen for outperformance. For example, solidity would be conveyed with evidence of history, track record and experience of partners. Innovation could be demonstrated with a focus on new ideas, techniques and processes delivered to industry-leading clients. Confidentiality may be illustrated with discretion about other clients. Framed awards on the walls might communicate achievement orientation. You cannot own all the virtues – focus on a distinctive dimension and deliver it.

Moving to positive – building trust

Trust is an unusual quality. Merely mentioning the word 'trust' can undermine it. Politicians for example use the word frequently and are among the least trusted groups in society. Paradoxically, if we consciously and openly ask for trust, that very question diminishes our ability to gain it. The subject thinks: why am I being asked for trust? To raise the issue in a personal relationship prejudices it. For example, celebrities signing a pre-nuptial agreement, in order to preserve their wealth lest the marriage fail, are almost inviting that failure. Research published by Bibb and Kourdi (2004) indicates that rather than speaking about trust, it is more effective to start quietly demonstrating it through providing progressive evidence of trustworthiness.

Trust builds naturally as reliability is demonstrated and commitments are kept. This takes time. The extended duration to build trust carries risks in a business context. Will the previous supplier win back the new customer? Will an alternative supplier tempt the new customers away before trust has been developed? I will show how to guard against this risk by accelerating the trust-building process. Act 3 engages the customer by building trust (see Figure A3.1).

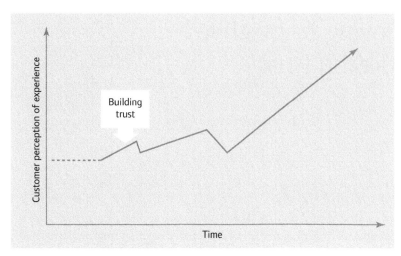

FIGURE A3.1 Satisfaction curve – building trust

Trust is the foundation

The economic value of trust was recognised when economist Muhammed Yunnus and the Grameen Bank won the 2006 Nobel Peace prize. An economist winning the Peace Prize (Foster, 2006) ahead of diplomats and politicians? True. Prosperity and peace are linked and Yunnus provided the basis for economic prosperity. In his own words, he realised that 'Charity is not the answer to poverty. It only helps poverty continue.' Aid simply creates dependency. His solution was to start at the bottom of the social pyramid. He lent small sums of money at commercial rates of interest to poor people in his native Bangladesh. There was no collateral and no credit rating. It was a gamble on trust. Since 1983, his Grameen bank has lent almost $6 billion with repayment rates exceeding 98%. Over 6 million people – 96% of them women – have become part of the global economy. And other micro-credit groups following his example in 100 countries have offered similar small loans to 92 million people. All based on trust.

The World Values Survey Association (WVSA), based in Stockholm, has conducted five waves of surveys between 1981 and 2007 covering 97 countries. WVSA has compared answers to questions such as: 'Do you think that generally strangers can be trusted?' The positive rate varies from 65% in Norway to about 5% in Brazil. Most countries scoring below 30% are locked in a suspicion-based poverty trap. According to Steve Knack, senior economist with the World Bank Development Research Group (quoted in Persaud, 2004), trust is one of the most powerful factors affecting a country's economic health – where trust is low, individuals and organisations are wary of engaging in financial transactions.

> where trust is low, individuals and organisations are wary of engaging in financial transactions

Where classical economists predicted the optimal value of trust between strangers as zero, the latest thinking places trust as a precursor to business success. The new neuro-economic theory about trust is that we have a fundamental biological need to trust one another. Paul Zak, neuro-scientist at Claremont Graduate University in California, holds the theory that human brains have evolved to cope with group living (Persaud, 2004). Previously psychologists have emphasised the model that intelligence is needed to outwit opponents for sex, food and status. There is a competitive urge certainly, but we also derive immense benefits from working together. Our brains have a strong social and co-operative adaptation.

Don't you love to be trusted?

Zak's research shows a correlation between trust and the presence of a hormone called oxytocin in our bodies. In a trustworthiness game, Zak discovered that oxytocin was not released when people trust others, but was instead released voluminously when others trust them. Persaud's summary is that 'It seems we love to be trusted – we find it deeply rewarding and tend to reciprocate with more generosity and more trust'. Biologically, we are programmed to trust if we are trusted.

Benefits of building trust online

Bringing the research into the twenty-first century, Wirz and Lihotzky (2003) have studied customer retention strategies of

Internet companies in B2C (business to consumer) electronic businesses. They chose this environment because barriers to customer switching are lower than in the traditional economy and vendors are more vulnerable to customer defections. The factors behind this are market transparency increased by the advent of smart shopping agents, the absence of physical distance between customers, suppliers and competitors, and the lack of personal customer–vendor relationships. They investigated different customer retention models, including trust building, community, convenience, free service and contractual agreements.

Trust leads to relationship commitment and increased commitment, because trust has a so-called echo effect, meaning that trust leads to more trust (unless misused), making trust itself a major driver of relationship stability. For Internet companies, achieving initial trust at the outset is harder because the customer has much less information to assess the trustworthiness of a supplier. There is no personal contact and it is not possible to assess the economic viability of an e-business from location, design and store size. Therefore electronic businesses use strong branding, certification, independent guarantees, flexible return policies, prompt and customer-orientated services and state-of-the-art complaint management. The findings of the research showed conclusively that companies operating a commerce-based business model were best served by a trust-building strategy.

So building trust is a demanding task that brings solid economic, psychological and commercial applications. How are companies actually behaving?

Where is the trust?

We know that trust comes partly from being trusted. Yet everywhere there are signs that companies do not trust their customers. Leisure centre swimming pools post plaques in big red block capitals all around the pool. These negative messages forbid behaviour that the majority would never contemplate. Petrol filling sites tell customers that the surveillance cameras will catch you if you drive off without paying (see Figure A3.2). Clothing retailers tag merchandise with heavy ink-tags to prevent theft. Office supply stores keep replacement printer cartridges in a locked glass case. Motels chain TV sets to the desk. Hotels warn that they will add the dressing gown to your bill if you steal it. Nightclubs lock their exits to prevent freeloading gatecrashers – with potentially tragic consequences in the event of fire. Paul Levesque labelled this the 'fortress mentality' (Levesque, 2006, pp. 93–95). These businesses treat customers as the greatest threat to their security. And if you show customers they are not trusted, how could they trust you in return?

if you show customers they are not trusted, how could they trust you in return?

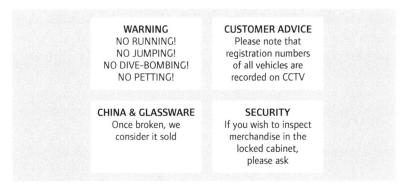

FIGURE A3.2 We do not trust you!

Of course, businesses need to take reasonable steps to guard against thieves. Yet what we know about trust makes it clear that treating the good 99% of customers distrustfully because of the bad 1% sends negative messages. Branding every customer a thief jettisons goodwill from the start. Better to make security measures less visible to customers. Vigilant store detectives operating discretely are a deterrent to thieves and unnoticed by the mass of customers. Pay particular attention to the signs on display. Ask yourself what message the red block capital **SECURITY** signs are giving to the good 99%. Do not destroy trust before the relationship has commenced.

Smart companies build trust …

Smart businesses know that good relationships are trust based and building trust is a service priority. It does not happen instantly in human relationships. When you meet a new person, you progressively validate your first impressions with observations based on subsequent behaviour to confirm (or otherwise) their trustworthiness. Picture yourself as young, free and seeking a partner … after meeting someone at a party you do not open a joint bank account the following morning. But you may learn to trust and love that person over a couple of years and end up married with joint finances. Trust takes time to grow and depends on consistently appropriate behaviour. Trust must be earned.

Likewise in customer relationships, trust takes time to develop. It results from reliable delivery of expectations, absence of unpleasant surprises, explanations for any shortfalls and consistent service quality.

… and do it rapidly

Time means risk with today's fickle customers. Allowing the process to unfold gradually over time may allow new customers to be tempted away by rival firms. So smart companies hasten the process with deliberate trust-building techniques. They know they have the reliability and service quality essential to justify trust.

They begin with research to understand the duration of the honeymoon period – the period when the experience has novelty for the customer. What is your equivalent of a politician's 'First 100 days'? How long do customers of your business need to gain confident familiarity? We are told that a new and unusual food must be tasted 12 times before it feels familiar. For an experience like Internet banking, it may take five iterations before the customer feels at ease. In a routine transaction at a new retail environment, two visits may suffice.

> smart companies observe the behaviour of cautious new customers

Smart companies observe the behaviour of cautious new customers. What are their worries? What do they say? How do they act? For example, you might hear customers say, 'Can you put that in writing?' or 'May I take your name, so I can refer to this conversation later?' These are danger signs that trust is missing. You need a trust-building process.

This process begins by understanding the cues and signals that show competence and build confidence. Use these insights to achieve and accelerate the natural process. For example, trust in a hotel is established through simple indications noticed in the first few minutes in the bedroom. Typically a guest will deposit a bag on the rack (is it stable?), wash and dry their hands in the bathroom (is the mirror smear-free and the towel white, soft and fluffy?) and switch on the TV (does it work?). Ensuring that these three 'trust tests' are passed means the mood of the guest is on an upward trajectory.

These businesses build credibility through indicators of competence and reliability.

Two more elements complete the picture. Trust often implies closeness. Finally, a critical component of genuine trust is the belief that the other party is acting reasonably and is not motivated by self-interest alone. These elements are combined in the equation below:

$$\text{trust} = \frac{\text{credibility} + \text{reliability} + \text{intimacy}}{\text{self-interest}}$$

Let us look at ten ways to build trust, as in Figure A3.3, beginning with self-interest.

FIGURE A3.3 Ten ways to build trust

Ten ways to build trust with new customers

1 'Put profit second'

Papyrus – a Swedish based international paper merchant – has found unbiased advice to be a powerful way of developing trust – especially when it saves money for customers. By helping customers find the most cost-effective product or the best deal, they are enhancing their long-term position. Similarly, George Merck, founder of the drug company of the same name, said in a speech in December 1950, 'We try never to forget that medicine is for the people. It is not for the profits. The profits follow, and if we have remembered that, they have never failed to appear. The better we have remembered it, the larger they have been' (quoted in Collins and Porras, 1994). He was recognised by *Fortune* magazine in 2003 as one of the ten greatest CEOs of all time under the headline 'George Merck put profit second'. Focus on the customers and not your own margins – and take care that customers come to notice this policy.

2 Check understanding, demonstrate listening

In the first contact with customers, ensure that the customer has correctly understood the information. Skills of active listening are important when a customer is providing information. This includes nods and short phases such as 'Right', 'Yes' or 'I see'. Writing down key facts or repeating them for confirmation also aids the process.

3 Progressive familiarisation

Planning for a staged process of understanding can be useful. Where services are complex, it may be most effective to arrange to cover the basics initially and then to add further information in bite-sized chunks.

4 Series of interactions

The experience of Papyrus shows that a series of short encounters, with reflection time in-between each, builds more confidence and trust than a single lengthy meeting. It may be possible to construct a set of welcome steps for a new customer to follow. For example, in business-to-business (B2B), you begin with a demonstration at the firm's premises, make a visit to a reference site subsequently and finally test the installation at their own location.

5 Personal contact

A named and identified person as a primary contact is reassuring. Or a business card with alternative numbers when help is required. We trust people who seem accessible and easy to reach. Handelsbanken offer a bespoke banking service which is not mass market. Each advisor has a small number of customers in order to give personal attention. There is no call centre and customers ring their branch directly.

6 Consistency over time and over media, between team members

Consistency is always a challenge. Customers rarely notice it. However, with eagle-eyes, they detect any inconsistencies. Brand standards are therefore critical for service organisations. Consider consistency from the customer's perspective. Watch how bank customers make longer lines behind smartly dressed tellers. The customers believe that tidy appearance correlates with professional performance. Yet in an architectural practice, clients may seek out the creative maverick. Consistency across media is also a challenge where web designers seek to depart from language, style and brand guidelines.

7 No surprises, nothing to hide

Openness and transparency are critical dimensions that contribute to a feeling of trustworthiness. 'No secrets' is a message customers like to hear. The skincare brand Elave promotes additive-free products with an advertising film where all the actors and actresses in the laboratory are naked to support the theme of 'nothing to hide'. Make transaction records accessible by customers, share internal data and offer back-up information.

8 Community commitment

Being a good citizen and a good neighbour creates a halo effect of trustworthiness. Allowing customers to discover charitable acts and considerate contributions to the community is more effective than overtly crowing about them. Sleep Country is Canada's leading bed retailer. When the company delivers new mattresses to customers in Ontario, the crew takes old ones away. These mattresses are evaluated and the gently used ones given to families in need, through their Donated Bed programme, which has been in operation for more than 12 years. In 2008 more than 20,000 of these gently used mattresses were provided to Ontario families in need.

9 Revealing something about you

Disclosure is a part of the process of getting to know others. Trust begins to develop when you open up about personal information. According to Chip Bell, author of *Magnetic Service* (2003), Universal Studios employees have their favourite film on their nametag. Some organisations have the service-giver's hometown on their nametag for the same reason – it humanises, gives a talking point, adds a dimension to the person providing the service. Revealing something personal about yourself is a sign of trust, which, when given, prompts trust in return.

10 Making and keeping many little promises

Customers cannot ascertain how effectively a service-provider will keep overall promises. However, they can form a view from the way the provider makes and keeps small promises in the initial period. For example, a commitment could be made to call a customer the next day at 3.00 p.m. Make the call at exactly 3.00 p.m. and refer to the promise. Undertake to supply drawings at the next meeting and begin the meeting with 'As promised, here are your drawings …'. Consider how many ways you could prove yourself with small promises about time and information.

> it is competent performance that builds trust

This final point may be the most critical one. It is competent performance that builds trust. Ensure that your early performance is exemplary, and an indicator of what is to come. Fairness, dependability, respect, openness, courage, unselfishness, empathy and compassion are all important attributes of trust (Bibb and Kourdi, 2004). All are needed, but in genuine trust building, think first of competence: how to deliver it AND how to demonstrate it in the early minutes, hours and days of the service experience.

HOW TO APPLY

Building trust: moving to positive

APPLICATION: MASS SERVICE

Airlines, banks, hotels, logistics, retailing, train-operating companies

Credibility through competence Smart uniforms build confidence. In retailing appearances build confidence. Pharmacists wear clean white coats. Beauticians have immaculate nails. Certificates of qualifications framed on the wall are an example. In travel companies ensure that passengers see small examples of competence. For example, witnessing the train manager removing litter left by a previous traveller reassures a new passenger that the environment is monitored. Hotels can show competence through the signs listed earlier in the chapter. Further examples are the folded corners of the outermost sheet of toilet roll, which shows that the toilet has been cleaned. A folded bathmat in the shower says that the cleaner has attended.

Accurate promises The timetable or schedule is a promise. When normal departure or arrival is delayed take care in making a new promise – to break one promise is disappointing, to break two is more serious. Should there be no information available (in uncertain weather for example), then an option is to advise the time of the next announcement and keep that promise.

Reliability Customers visit one branch to make preliminary enquiries, reflect and then may proceed with the transaction at another branch. Inconsistent standards will be discovered. This can affect franchise

▶

retailers like Benetton where customers buy an item from the range of one outlet and find it cannot be returned at another franchisee selling other Benetton ranges.

Looking safe, being safe Make customers feel safe. Passengers place their security in the hands of the operator. Consequently it is important that passengers, especially first-time or infrequent travellers, see that safety and security are being treated as a priority. Remember that someone is hearing this standard safety briefing for the first time; think ofs them as you deliver the familiar words. Furthermore, note that repetitive routines give comfort to the nervous.

No surprises The unexpected can be disturbing. When a plane takes off at night, cabin lights are dimmed. Warn passengers a minute beforehand. In a hotel, prepare guests for fire alarm tests.

Gestures of generosity Small gestures of generosity can make a significant difference. Le Creuset kettles are expensive. But when the whistle ceases to sound, the company provides a replacement free of charge. For the customer it feels unexpectedly good. Le Creuset management understand that without the whistle the customer may buy a new kettle, which might tempt them away from the Le Creuset brand.

APPLICATION: SERVICE SHOP

Hospitals, car repairers, travel agents

Trust building Service industry research in the travel industry has shown that two factors impact on trust building. The first factor is person-related, where customers' willingness to trust a firm is influenced by empathy, politeness and the similarity between customer and company representative – we tend to trust people like ourselves. The second factor is offer-related and trust here derives from indicators of customisation, competence, reliability and promptness. Time is another factor, with the length of the relationship influencing the degree of trust.

Credibility through cleanliness Everyone knows that hospitals must be clean. Therefore hygiene and perceptions of cleanliness are fundamental. The hospital should be designed to look clean with good waste systems, facilities for dirty food plates and dirty sheets to be out of sight, plus regular cleaning that is noticed by the patients and visitors. Provide different colour aprons for medical and catering roles. Make cleanliness noticeable – NHS hospitals provide hand-gel for visitors to cleanse hands before entering the wards with reminders to encourage use.

Car franchises know that a clean and tidy forecourt makes a strong first impression.

No surprises Patient information packs show the timeline of the processes and steps. Diagrams help patients and their carers visualise what will happen to them at each stage.

Fairness Perceptions of fairness matter. When hospitals add warnings on appointment letters that patients who fail to attend appointments twice lose their place, we should not be surprised if there is anger when appointments are deferred twice.

Empathy and intimacy Why do some doctors get sued and others do not? Wendy Levinson MD recorded hundreds of conversations between doctors and their patients to answer this. The conclusion was three minutes. In a 1997 *Journal of the American Medical Association* study (Levinson *et al.*, 1997), primary care physicians who had never faced a malpractice suit spent an average of only 3.3 minutes more per patient interview (18.3 compared with 15 minutes for those who had faced a malpractice suit). They were also more outwardly caring, tending to make comments that involved the patient in what was happening, such as, 'First, I'll examine you, and then we'll talk over your problem'. In fact the quality of medical information given was equal. It was about listening actively. The way they showed empathy made the difference. (Information on the research of Wendy Levinson is also available in Butler and Keller, 1999, and Gladwell, 2006.)

Accountants, architects, consultants, doctors, lawyers

Professionalism Professional advisors must of course appear professional in their dress and demeanour. They must also show a professional interest in keeping up-to-date. This can be expressed through sharing relevant information with clients and keeping them abreast of industry developments.

Core requirement What is the one core element of your professional service you must deliver to underline credibility? For an architectural practice, it will be the effective design and soundness of the office building. For an accountancy practice, there must be a sense of organised order about appointments, phone calls and meetings. Legal firms must double-check letters and ensure each line is error free. For an advertising agency, there needs to be an atmosphere of creativity delivered.

Credibility The perceptions created by the tangible evidence contribute to the early impressions of trustworthiness. How is the telephone answered? Is the reception area orderly? A display of awards and external endorsements can all add quality to the first impressions. Details of professional qualifications count too.

Proof of dependability In professional services, it is difficult to demonstrate the reliability of the service before the outcomes are delivered, normally occurring at the end of the process. For this reason, there is a paramount need to give minor examples of meeting commitments at each interaction. Every client phone call and meeting should feature an action that was promised at the last encounter. Letters should convey promises kept. Although it is never stated in so many words, the silent message is 'we keep our promises'.

Consistency Customers want the reassurance of consistency. In professional services, this can only be delivered by harmonious behaviour between team members. Consultants, or lawyers, or accountants need to take care that they do not contradict each other. Each team member should know and reinforce the messages given by other contacts. Show that you are in harmony and in touch with who spoke to them the previous time.

Queues and bad news – reality check

Every parent knows the 20-second rule. When a young child asks to go to the swimming pool today, you have no more than 20 seconds to say 'no' and have it accepted. Delay your answer longer than this and the child has already created a picture in their mind of happy splashing. A delayed refusal can result in tears and tantrums. If the answer is 'yes', you can take your time over saying it. The anticipation may even increase the pleasure. But if you have to say no, or give out bad news, you must move swiftly. We are going to apply this insight to the service encounter so that we manage the customer's emotions through the process.

Act 4 is a reality check. Your customer may have unrealistic hopes. You may have legitimate constraints. Any gap between customer expectations and what you can deliver carries risks to the long-term. This act is about closing the gap with a reality check. And doing it early in the process (see Figure A4.1).

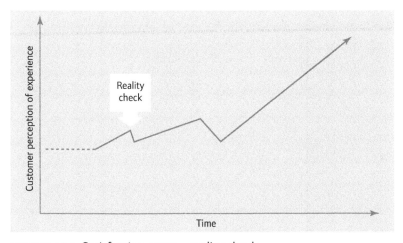

FIGURE A4.1 Satisfaction curve – reality check

Let's be realistic

It is so easy for reality to fall short of our hopes. Somehow we seem to be slightly optimistic. We expect to arrive a little earlier than actually happens. We fail to allow for all the details. There is often a mismatch between expectations and actuality, and when the rude awakening occurs, we face disappointment. And the longer the unrealistic expectation goes on, the harder it hurts to be disappointed.

> the longer the unrealistic expectation goes on, the harder it hurts to be disappointed

This happens in the minds of our customers. Their expectations may go beyond what we can reasonably deliver. So we must carry out the reality check as quickly as possible so that their hopes are founded on reality and can be met. We must address unrealistic customer demands early in the process. Let us correct potential misunderstandings before they occur.

Place good news second

There is a second reason why the reality check has to come early. It may carry with it some bad news. Imagine that you have two pieces of information to impart. You are tempted to blurt out the best news first. It is exciting and you know the listener will enjoy it. This is tempting – and wrong. The professional newsreaders know better. Watch how they save the good news to the end of the broadcast and leave the audience on a positive note. If you go straight in with the good news, the only way from there is downwards. Ask your boss which they want first and they will say the same:

I've got some good news and some bad news. Which do you want first?

Let's get the bad news over and done with. Save the good news to the end, please.

Years ago when children's vaccination injections were painful, the parents used to save a sweet to give the child afterwards. Make sure that you have something good to follow any setback the customer may experience. Remove misconceptions early in the process and sequence bad news before good news.

Clustering bad news

There is a third nuance to this process. As well as bringing bad news in at an early stage in the process, we must also consider the framing of the human mind. Bad news is an unpopular message. How can we mitigate this? Machiavelli understood the threat to Princes and advised them to bundle all the bad news together in one fell swoop:

> *Severities should be dealt out all at once, so that their suddenness may give less offence.*

> *Benefits ought to be handed out drop by drop, so that they may be relished the more.*

> Niccolo Machiavelli

Was he the first political spin-doctor? You may suspect company CEOs of following the same approach in their dealings with investors. If the firm is having a bad financial year, perhaps they may bring forward any potential bad news from the coming year, to make this year dreadful … And thereby be well placed to have a good following year.

On the other hand, people enjoy hearing good news. Research by Chase and Dasu (2001) concludes that when you have a number of elements of good news, it is better to space them throughout the service experience. For example, best practice in a 12-month consulting assignment is to segment the process into stages and to celebrate the attainment of each milestone during the year. Ikea spreads its offers of the week along the pathway shoppers must follow with good deals sprinkled throughout the store.

BEST PRACTICE

A reality check must come early in the process

Looking first at the reality check, what does this mean in practice?

It demands that you look actively for signs that things may be going awry. These may be visible clues, like frowning, or standing up and pacing. Are customers grumbling to unrelated staff or other customers? You should check directly. Witness how, in the best restaurants, the waiting staff will glide up to your table, within three minutes of serving your main course and ask discretely, 'Is everything all right with your meal?' They allow you just enough time to see the presentation, taste the flavour and assess the dish. If you answer 'yes', they place you in a positive frame of mind. If there is any disappointment or misunderstanding they can put matters right and still end on a positive note. Leaving it longer than this may result in your complaining when it is too late to rectify the problem.

The most frequent disappointments that occur in service businesses are related to customer expectations of the cost of the service, the service quality or the waiting time.

Correcting price perceptions

The financial aspects should be addressed by care in advertising and by better use of price signals or effective pre-communication of price scales. Low-cost airlines have come under pressure to display total prices in advertisements rather than come-on prices, which are subject to surcharges for baggage, taxes and payment by credit card. Ryanair needed to close its website for a couple of days in early 2008 in order to install software to clarify total flight costs. Another answer is to provide basic propositions for the more price-sensitive customers and upscale offers for less price-sensitive customers. Presenting a choice at an early stage avoids price disappointment.

> presenting a choice at an early stage avoids price disappointment

The simple act of making a choice involves the customer in the decision, so that there is less likely to be a challenge later.

In tougher economic times, premium prices come under pressure from customers. Figure A4.2 shows two options for response: lowering the perceived price or improving the service, enhancing the emotional value or using better communication to convey the quality more effectively.

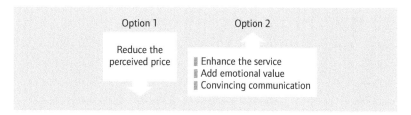

FIGURE A4.2 Responding to price concerns

UK supermarket Waitrose saw sales decline in late 2008 and identified a strong pressure from consumers for better value. Waitrose's commercial director Richard Hodgson said, 'Our research suggest many of our shoppers do not think they can do a full weekly shop at Waitrose on a tight budget. We have found some customers putting their Waitrose goods in Tesco bags, because they are nervous that their neighbours will think they are decadent for shopping at Waitrose.' Other customers had deserted the upmarket store for hard discount stores such as Aldi and Lidl. Average items per basket had dropped by one item. The response in March 2009 was to launch the Waitrose Essentials range – 800 everyday food and grocery products at everyday affordable prices in simple white packaging. After six months, sales of the re-priced and repackaged items had increased by 17% with £100 million total sales. A further vindication of the launch was that average number of items per basket had risen by two products. Overall sales figures outperformed rival retailers and by demonstrating their understanding of customers' expectations of value, they were rewarded with market share gains.

A particular risk zone arises when a customer has experienced a bargain offer at the previous transaction. This can set a perception of an expected future price. Where a business offers an introductory discount, it is appropriate to educate customers about long-term benchmark prices. Where customers may challenge prices with a lower price paid last time, it is important that staff are briefed to confirm prices at an early stage, or at least provide an estimate or an agreed basis for charging. The aim is to ensure that there is no nasty surprise later.

Correcting quality perceptions

Sampling, taster packs or trial offers can ensure that the customer is prepared for the standard of the regular package. Naturally these must be representative. Misunderstandings and apparent shortfalls in quality can be addressed with early perception checks and instant feedback techniques. Management consultants refer to this as 'time-out' and ask to review the process with the client to flush out any emerging concerns.

Correcting time perceptions

Time-based assumptions are more difficult to address because in most services there will be variability. Demand and capacity are difficult to match in most services for reasons of demand variability, seasonality and inability to flex capacity and resources at short notice. Service providers can use techniques to influence demand such as communicating busy and quiet times via signs and advertising to encourage/discourage use. You can incentivise some customers to come or call at quiet times. You can also flex capacity by recruiting part-time employees, adding overtime working, subcontracting or outsourcing. The supermarket Sainsbury's uses electronic sensors to track people coming into each store to schedule checkout staff. Incoming numbers give an indication of queuing peaks occurring 10–20 minutes later. Nevertheless, when demand exceeds supply, the consequence is customers waiting.

> incentivise some customers to call at quiet times

Customers regard waiting as wasted time; they find it frustrating. It leads to disappointment and dissatisfaction. Empty or unoccupied time feels oppressive. They feel powerless, at the mercy of the server. Research suggests that consumers on average significantly over-estimate how long they have been waiting. Subjective or perceived time is felt to be greater than objective time as measured by the clock.

While customers are waiting, they may move into a negative frame of mind and start to notice other shortfalls. When the customer is waiting on the phone, they re-read the letter and spot the typographical errors. In the store, they gaze around and see the stain on the carpet or the missing light bulb. Thoughts move on to the next activity and customers resent the delay, expressing it as time theft as in Figure A4.3.

'You are stealing
MY time!'

FIGURE A4.3 Waiting …

You may lose their business. A *Wall Street Journal* survey by Emily Nelson (2000) reported that 83% of women and 91% of men said that long checkout queues had prompted them to stop using a particular store. On the other hand, McDonalds has determined that sales increase by 1% for every six seconds consumers save in using the drive through window.

Waiting is clearly a critical dimension in service businesses. How should we respond?

Queues and waiting time

Success comes from a combination of minimising the objective time that customers wait and also influencing the perceptions of subjective time. There are ten techniques to manage queuing impressions:

1 Accelerate

Ensure that customers have all the information they need. While they are waiting on the phone, a recorded message reminds Direct Line customers to have ready their policy number. Give checklists to customers. Pre-warn them of the sequence of questions they will be asked. Retail stores play fast tempo music at peak times to encourage shoppers to walk more quickly. UPS agents all seem to speak quickly and mirroring theory says that this encourages customers to speed up in return.

2 Anticipate

Make customers feel that the service has somehow already started. Some restaurants give waiting customers a menu to choose from, or even take their order. BUPA hospitals offering regular screening programmes give arriving patients a sample bottle to fill and a medical card to complete, so that the initial wait appears to be part of the process.

3 Automate

Carry out some activities automatically or pre-authorise so that transactions go through quickly. The Amazon 'one-click' payment system uses pre-authorisation. British Airways encourages passengers to check-in online and to print their own boarding passes before they arrive at the airport. Credit-scoring customers *before* they ask to borrow money means that bank loans can be pre-approved.

Buffering can reduce the delays that customers cause others behind them. For example, it can be frustrating when the person at the front of the queue fumbles in a purse for change. The two-sided cash register addresses this. The cashier sits in the middle of two alternating lines. While the left queue customer is being served, the right queue customer can prepare himself. Then as the left queue customer packs up her purchases, the cashier swings to deal with the right queue customer. No one is delayed by another customer. Drive-through restaurants ask customers to place an order at one window and pick up at another partly to give customers an activity in the meantime so that the perceived wait is minimised.

4 Discriminate

Identify and separate out the most valuable customers. Frequent customers or high-spending customers can be given priority in service. Airlines fast-track business-class travellers. The supermarket Tesco discovered from ClubCard data that its most valuable customers tended to shop on Thursday evenings. The company now rosters their smartest, fastest checkout staff for these times to ensure the best customers get the most efficient service. Fidelity, the investment business, uses an assessment of client net worth to prioritise phone answering. Using phone number recognition systems, the company ensures that calls from high-value and high-potential clients are picked up on the third ring. Lower-value customers receive a more variable service and often ring for longer.

Segregate customers with complex needs and direct them to highly skilled agents, while the other agents deal with standard requirements. Greeters can assess customer needs and direct them to the right line.

Offer a reservation service to guarantee that the service will be available when the customer arrives. It shifts some demand to the off-peak times, but risks the problem of lost capacity through no-shows. The answer of overbooking can lead to disappointed and delayed customers.

5 Reallocate

Phone queues at busy times can be addressed by offering customers lower down the queue, the opportunity to leave a phone number to be called back at an agreed time. Even customers who turn down this option feel empowered – they are now queuing by choice. Recorded messages can detail quieter times and this may persuade some customers to reallocate themselves away from the peak on this occasion or in future. You can highlight another channel of communication. LloydsTSB Bank encourages phone bank customers to use Internet banking to save time.

6 Animate

Distract customers. Some businesses show advertising films like the UK Post Office. You can use music in shops, lifts, on phone lines. Importantly, you should research your customers' tastes – UK insurance brand leader Direct Line assumes all their customers like old Frank Sinatra songs.

Rather than playing old music, Southwest Airlines uses an animated recorded message. When customers call 1–800 IFLYSWA a spoken monologue by an enthusiastic staff member distracts them during the wait. The recording explains that the team is busy and will be with you soon and then poses a rapid-fire series of questions: 'Are you near a window? Can you see outside? How is the weather? Do you have any plans for later? Are you going to a movie? What was the last film you saw? Who starred in it? What other films have they made?' The caller's mind is absorbed with interesting thoughts about themselves, instead of annoyed thoughts about the company keeping them waiting.

Live music is better still – could you hire a pianist at peak times? Or how about free drinks – Peter Russell, a Hertfordshire butcher, plies his queue of Christmas customers with cups of hot coffee. Restaurants provide nibbles for waiting guests.

A higher quality environment is better with more comfortable chairs and softer floor carpet. Mirrors are marvellous. Banks use them to disguise waiting time, so do hotels in their foyers and elevators. Narcissistic customers can admire their reflections. Voyeurs can surreptitiously scrutinise their fellow customers. Some women secretly scan the shoes of those around them.

7 Obfuscate

Manage perceptions with a progress bar that moves slowly at first (underestimating actual progress) and then speeds up at the end. Or disguise the true length of the queue and exaggerate the time it will take. Then 'over-deliver' by claiming to give a customer priority or by announcing extra capacity to speed up the process. The aim is to appear as the hero shortening the wait. A caveat – this is inadvisable for businesses with repeat customers. In my view misleading customers is always risky and generally unwise (it breaches trust).

8 Alleviate

Remove anxiety by identifying and addressing customer concerns. Explain that the order is not lost. Tell them that they are next in line. Acknowledge them by eye – a simple technique that barmen use in busy pubs. You can utilise the Scandinavian number system, where arriving customers pull off a ticket from a roll and come to the counter when the screen displays their number. Text-based systems are now available to allow customers to roam and to be reminded when their time is nigh.

Alternatives to the number roll queuing system are the single-line queue and the multi-line queue. The single-line queue is fairer but operationally slower (since there is a lag time in a multi-line system while customers walk from their queue to the desk). The multi-line system allows customers to pick the line that looks the shortest or fastest and join another queue that moves more swiftly, so it offers the benefit of choice.

9 Educate

Give demonstrations of other products. Use the time to train customers in product application or show new potential. Give them background about the product, service, history and production process. Coffee shops have wall posters detailing the history of coffee growing or the process of selecting coffee beans. If these facts are memorably presented they occupy the mind and may even lead to word-of-mouth repetition to potential customers.

▶

10 Participate

Involve them in the activity. US supermarket Kroger Co introduced self-scanning in 20 stores in Louisville, Kentucky in 1997 and customers using this system believe that it takes less time than queuing at the checkout. Domino Pizza's website allows people to trace the progress of their order, including the name of the cook and the delivery person along with the expected time of arrival.

BEST PRACTICE

Phone waiting time

Phone waiting time is a substantial frustration for many service customers. Efficient companies minimise the cost of idle staff and deliberately under-recruit call centre staff, knowing that running a permanent queue will have all agents working the whole day. Although this is commercially sensible for the company and relevant for the cost-conscious customer, it is frustrating the moment the customer has a query to resolve. Unsurprisingly many customers take out their frustration in the form of phone rage. Abused agents resign their call centre jobs. High churn means that customers are often answered by inexperienced agents. It is a challenging situation.

The best practices can mitigate but not solve this challenge:

1 Honesty with waiting customers

Rather than a standard recorded message saying this is 'a particularly busy time', be truthful and provide a time-band during which the caller is likely to be answered. For example, set expectations of say a three-minute wait. Then endeavour to provide staff numbers to deliver an answer within this time.

2 Advise customers of progress

Sophisticated telephone systems are able to inform customers at the outset that they are say 20th in line for an answer. Further updates illustrate how they are moving up the queue to 10th, and so on. It also gives an incentive to hang on, instead of ringing off and starting again.

3 Messages should be spoken by a brand ambassador

This means a young brand should have a youthful voice, a prestige brand should have an authoritative voice. The mobile phone operator, Orange, has chosen a young, feisty character for their recorded messages in keeping with the brand identity. The vocabulary should fit with the brand imagery. Music should be in keeping with the brand and the tastes of typical customers.

4 Avoid obvious messages

Telling people they are 'in a queue and will be answered as soon as an agent becomes available' increases frustration. Callers obviously understand all to well that they are in a queue! They have phoned before. Phrases like 'Your custom is important to us' aggravates because waiting makes them feel unimportant and the phrase underlines this.

5 Do not repeat the message too frequently

Disney do not remind theme park visitors that they are in a queue for Thunder mountain every 20 seconds!

Phone waiting is also an issue in service businesses without call centre agents. Switchboards take calls that cannot be put through immediately. Operators should not say 'I am putting you on hold'. Instead they should always seek permission. The phrase, 'May I put you on hold?' is better. Best of all is to ask 'Are you able to hold?' The clear message is that the caller's time is respected. At the end of the wait, the standard response is the apology, 'Sorry to keep you waiting', which draws attention to the negative side of waiting. A smarter response is to return with 'Thank you for waiting', which is positive.

BEST PRACTICE

Difficulties and bad news to be covered early

If there is any part of the service experience that is awkward, arduous or unpleasant, it is better to phase it as early as possible in the encounter. This allows time and opportunity later in the process to recover, impress and delight.

Envisage the situation where a customer needs a replacement refrigerator. The retail assistant demonstrates the range and helps the customer take into account the capacity required, the available width in the kitchen, the features and facilities that are needed. Finally the customer chooses in confidence, only to be told that this model is out of stock. Superior thinking comes from the UK retailer Argos, which allows customers to check the availability of catalogue items early in the search process and before placing a counter order. This brings forward any potential disappointment, allowing the customer and the store time to find an alternative and end on a better note.

Partitioned or all-inclusive prices?

Some headline prices are partitioned – meaning that the price is not all-inclusive. Partitioned prices show prices for products or services with tax or shipping costs listed separately. In some cases the extra elements of a partitioned price are revealed late in the process and the customer does not discover the additional costs until the invoicing stage. Digital media expert Andrew Walmsley cites a two-year research study of online retailing and delivery costs. The conclusion warns against the tendency to spring costs on buyers at the checkout. Retailers who are perceived as not being straight about their charges leave a bad taste in the consumer's mouth. As one interviewee put it, 'You think you're spending £10 and suddenly it's £13.'

Consumers believe prices should include tax – in Australian retail pricing it is a legal requirement. Best practice also demands that any required additions are clarified early.

> ## the customer needs to feel that they have been treated fairly

The customer needs to feel that they have been treated fairly. Positive examples are banks that credit-score loan applications early in the discussion so that borrowing expectations are founded on realism. Any uncomfortable procedure in a medical examination should be described at the outset and if practical, be undertaken in the early phases. This minimises the minutes of dread beforehand. In professional services, new clients may have a particular partner or consultant in mind. If this is not feasible, they should be made aware of the reasons and be introduced to the proposed contact quickly, rather than being allowed to continue with an unrealistic hope.

Addressing difficulties early gives you the longest time to recover and allows the latter parts of the experience to create a positive and lasting final impression.

BEST PRACTICE

Other customers behaving badly

Dealing with difficulties early has an additional aspect in services performed in the presence of other customers. Examples are restaurants, theatres and public transport. These providers must take into account the impact of customers on each other. Inconsiderate behaviour by one customer or group of customers can severely damage the experience for other patrons. For example, British Airways cabin crew are carefully trained to intervene early in a flight if a passenger is disrupting the enjoyment of other travellers. Initially a discrete and courteous warning will be given, explaining what is acceptable and why. If this remains unheeded, firm and stern measures will follow to bring the passenger into line. Other passengers see that their needs are being recognised by the airline. ▶

Smart firms encourage and educate customers to behave more considerately. There are nine techniques:

1 Service design

Aim to design the service so one customer cannot spoil it for others. The airline Ryanair has installed fixed seating in its aircraft, partly because passengers were irritated by reclined seats from the passenger in front (and partly so that Ryanair can fit more seats into their budget flight planes).

2 Focus on first-time customers

Try to identify and brief new customers on how to get the best out of the service. A restaurant with a particular dress code will ask, 'Have you dined here before?' when they receive a call to book a table. If the answer is no, then a polite explanation will be given that gentlemen should wear a tie.

3 Communicate behaviour standards

Educate or remind customers on how they should act during the service. As patrons take their seats at Cineworld, they see a cartoon with a Lara Croft lookalike who deals drastically with noisy talkers, smokers and users of mobile phones in order to teach people how to make the experience pleasant for other filmgoers. Airlines show safety films before take-off. And to ensure passengers pay close attention, Air New Zealand's safety video for its domestic routes shows a pilot and cabin crew dressed only in body paint made to resemble their normal uniforms.

4 Use one customer to influence new patrons

Is it possible to introduce a new customer to an existing buyer who acts as mentor? Software providers may invite new buyers into a user group where existing customers can explain and answer questions on how to make the best use of helplines and company advisors. Fellow customers may be better placed than the software provider to counsel patience with expert technical staff.

5 Allow customers to rate each other

Develop an internal market where customers interact with each other. eBay uses a star-rating system where buyers rate sellers. Naturally sellers want to build a 'good reputation' so they have every incentive to treat purchasers honestly and fairly.

6 Reminders

Display signs to remind people of correct behaviour. In the UK, long-distance rail operators offer quiet carriages on their services. Window stickers have graphic illustrations of a mobile phone with a red diagonal prohibition sign across it. Witty newspaper correspondence from *The Times* on the subject of considerate and inconsiderate behaviour in railway carriages could be reproduced and framed for customers to read and be reminded.

7 Staff training

Train staff to make transgressors aware of their shortcomings. As noted above, British Airways teach cabin crew techniques to address customer inconsideration in a non-confrontational way. Some organisations find that older or more senior people are better placed to carry out this function. Role playing regularly gives staff confidence to tackle issues as they arise.

8 Penalise customers for bad behaviour

A North American store selling female clothing identified a customer returning 80% of her purchases and ceased selling to her because the time taken to check and re-rack the items had the effect of reducing service for other customers. Hairdressers restrict appointments to less busy times for customers who irritate regular clients. However, penalties may not change behaviour. Levitt and Dubner's book *Freakonomics* (2005) cites a nursery that began fining parents for late collections of their toddlers. The parents' timekeeping actually deteriorated because they were willing to pay for lateness. Penalties need to be tested to ensure that they improve behaviour rather than legitimising bad behaviour.

▶

9 Sack bad customers

In the final analysis, the enjoyment of the majority of customers is likely to be worth more in repeat business and recommendation than the profit from one inconsiderate person. The hotel chain Premier Inn commits to a money-back guarantee should a guest fail to get a good night's sleep. They create a quiet, comfortable environment but this can be ruined by a noisy guest late at night. Where they identify guests who disturb others, the hotel first issues a warning and ultimately takes no further accommodation bookings from them. Other hotel chains have a policy not to take bookings from film crews because experience illustrates that their unsocial hours can disrupt the positive experience of other guests.

People make the service experience, and this can go beyond employees to include the other customers. Part of a positive service encounter is the atmosphere created by other users. Smarter service providers consider the impact of other guests. Niche service businesses now take pains to target and select their customers and exclude the non-harmonious. Mass market operators are considering how best to educate their customers in mutual consideration.

You don't need to be perfect, you just have to show you are taking responsibility and you are trying to persuade one customer to be respectful of others.

BEST PRACTICE

Cluster any bad news together

In consumer television programmes relating to customer service, the horror stories seem to have many chapters to them and each episode carries with it an additional failure or piece of bad news. Just when you think it cannot get any worse, the experience takes another downward step! By contrast, the perfect approach ensures that anything and everything negative will be addressed early, as in Figure A4.4. Any awkward or difficult aspects of the service experience need to be clustered together. The benefit of this approach is that the customer has a stronger recollection of the later positive aspects of the experiences. Any negatives have been overtaken by positive feelings.

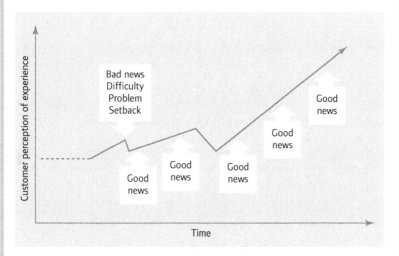

FIGURE A4.4 Bad news once, good news often

Plan the service encounter. Specifically, consider all potential difficulties that can arise from the customer's viewpoint. It may be waiting time, perhaps some kind of physical or financial assessment, it may be physical or emotional pain, possibly a form of rejection or refusal, or an answer that is not welcomed. Consider how to cluster the difficulties and amalgamate all the delays into one episode. For example, it is better to queue once for a longer period than to discover that a second queue follows the first one. Inbound phone callers are often offered a menu of numbered options: press 1 for a new claim, press 2 for an existing claim, for example. It is better to offer fewer menus with more choices, than to give a couple of choices each time and demand that customers work their way through four, five or six menus before reaching the correct call agent or department. Make the final item on the menu a repeat of the choices. A smaller number of stages are perceived as more customer friendly. The UK Passport Agency is a government-run service that exemplifies best practice in recorded menu design and effective service delivery.

Some customers see questions as hurdles when they just want to get on with the service. Therefore include an explanation of why you are asking the question: 'I need to know this so I can give you the best advice'. Let customers know how many questions are to be asked or how many minutes it will take. Say what will follow so that they can look forward to that.

BEST PRACTICE

Spread good news throughout the encounter

Customers have unlimited capacity for good news and therefore it should be partitioned so that elements of good news occur throughout the process, culminating in the final *pièce de résistance*, of course. Small positive surprises can be placed along the route, just like the child's Easter egg hunt where a tiny chocolate egg is found with every clue leading to the giant chocolate egg at the end. Positive phases can be spread through the encounter. When a passenger is upgraded for the first time, let them discover the variety of delights over the duration of the flight. This has more impact than hearing all the benefits at the outset.

With the reality check completed and any potentially negative elements resolved you are ready to take the trajectory onwards and upwards.

HOW TO APPLY

Reality check: earlier is better

APPLICATION: MASS SERVICE

Airlines, banks, hotels, logistics firms, retailing, train-operating companies

Queues and waiting time Queues are frustrating to travellers. Fear of missing a flight or a train can bring out negative emotions in customers; so accurate pre-information and responsive handling of customers is needed. It is reassuring to demonstrate that the queue is being handled fairly and competently. Airports give checklists to prepare passengers for security checks. Airlines ask travellers at the gate to be ready to show their boarding card and have their passport open at the page with the photograph. Both of these tactics encourage passengers to be prepared so that they do not delay other travellers.

Station queues to buy train tickets can be enhanced by distractions such as brochures and leaflets to read. Those waiting are willing to be distracted with information, offers and advertising, but the material must be interesting and stimulating. Captivate the attention of a passenger who would otherwise be grumbling mentally about the time delay – most ticket office communications fall short of this obvious objective.

Hotel queues for check-in and checkout are negatively perceived by guests, yet the flows peaking at busy times mean waiting is often inevitable. The bartender's technique of catching the eye of the next patron with a signal of acknowledgement is reassuring to that person and also those further back in the queue. It says that the check-in clerk is aware of the time pressures. The phrase 'Thanks for waiting' is more positive than an apology because it shows gratitude and encourages patience further down the queue.

Retail queues can be minimised through accurate assessments of customer flow and adequate staffing. When unexpected queues build up, a loudspeaker announcement calling extra staff to the tills conveys a positive message. Showing responsiveness is important. Queuing distractions can reduce customer frustration. Some UK post offices have screens showing advertisements to distract queuing customers.

In a bank, where every teller position is manned, customers feel that the best efforts are being made to meet demand. Conversely customers resent seeing back-office staff handling paperwork when the queues are long and some positions are unfilled.

Fairness perceptions Customers dislike multiple-line queues for fear that they will make the slow choice. Many high volume retailers such as Marks & Spencer and Tesco Express are moving over to single lines. Measured with a stop-watch, the lag time between a customer moving from the head of the line to the first available till means that service is slower under this system compared with multiple lines. However, customer perceptions of equity and steady progress mean that the single-line approach is often preferable.

Empathy Phone banks may frustrate customers with a lengthy wait for a short transaction. First Direct train their agents in 'polite disengagement' so that calls with garrulous customers can be curtailed with no offence, releasing agents to handle the next caller. Finally, where customers have experienced a long wait, a powerful approach is honest appreciation of the patience when the call is eventually picked up: 'Thanks for your patience'.

Bad news early For an airline, part of the customer promise is safe transport of baggage. If, for any reason, some bags have not been loaded, the right time to tell the passengers is early in the journey. Leaving passengers in ignorance for a final letdown in the baggage hall is a soft option for cabin crews who know that someone else will take the pressure when their duties are completed. Early notice means that some compensatory consideration can be provided on board and the customer can work out the consequences and actions required on arrival. It may also be the case that the pilot knows in advance that baggage handling on arrival will be slow and can pre-warn passengers. Give bad news early.

For a retailer, customers can be frustrated when popular items are out of stock or have restricted availability. Best practice is to warn customers as early as possible. For example, at launch, iPhones were limited to one per customer and notices about this were on display at the store doors.

Service disruption Trains, planes, ferries and buses operate to a schedule which is effectively a 'time promise' to passengers. Therefore delay and service disruption feels like a broken promise. The first answer is to resource and train for reliability. But inevitably disruptions will occur, so the second answer is to give the earliest warning of any service failure, so that passengers may prepare or take alternative action. Give bad news as quickly as practicable. Also identify likely implications and be ready to provide responses to these. For example, a late arrival may not preclude a connection being made. The third answer is to keep customers up-to-date as the situation unfolds. Finally, for a passenger, the delay may be a serious problem. Therefore make clear that the organisation realises the seriousness – placing senior managers on the concourse of a station or an airport is one way to show this.

Hospitals, car repairers, travel agents

Empathy Consider the recruitment and selection process. Recruit people who can share the feelings of patients or customers. Ask on your application form for an example of 'how you helped someone in the past seven days'. If potential recruits cannot provide credible instances from recent experience, perhaps they are the wrong person to work in this role.

Information Setting expectations about waiting time reduces uncertainty and allows people to sit back rather than waiting on the edge of their chair. Knowing if it may be more than 30 minutes ensures less anxiety than an open-ended wait. Travel agents can guide holidaymakers on the right time length to allow for flight check-in and security so that anxiety is avoided.

Hospital queues and waiting time For patients in hospitals waiting can be an anxious time. Those waiting may fear bad news. They dread physical pain or the prospect of inconvenience or discomfort. Distractions in waiting areas can provide a palliative. The norm is to provide magazines and journals. Check they are current. However, many customers feel unable to concentrate on reading. There are more creative approaches. How about shoals of colourful tropical fish circling by? What about an art show – maybe a school or university art department is willing and even eager to lend display works.

Hospital fairness In hospital Accident and Emergency areas, display a sign saying: 'Patients are seen in the order of clinical need.' This eases resentment from apparent unfairness for delayed patients who are seen out of sequence.

Impact of other patients In hospitals, other patients can cause much distress. Be aware of the annoyance of inconsiderate parking. Picture the embarrassment from overhearing confidential consultations. Imagine the frustration late at night of lying near to another patient snoring loudly. Think of the tension felt by an asthmatic patient passing the crowd of smokers outside the hospital entrance.

Handling bad news in hospital Breaking bad news to people is difficult. Those needing to pass on bad tidings need training in skills and appreciation of best practices. Role plays can prepare people on how to give information and how to give support. The news of the heart bypass operation is worse than the heart attack. A successful approach in hospitals is the 'Patient's Friend' scheme where those who are about to undergo heart surgery meet people who have been through the experience. They are able to question them about their fears and concerns. Members of such a coronary aftercare group need appropriate training.

Handling bad news in car repair and travel agencies
For car repairers, the initial diagnosis can seem like bad news to the customer, particularly if the mechanical repair is going to be expensive or take time. Certainly, the information should be imparted as speedily as possible. It should also be expressed positively. For example, the customer could be told, 'Timing chain – it is a big job, it'll cost you hundreds and we don't have the parts in stock.' How much better to hear, 'Good news, we've identified the problem before it caused expensive damage to your car, so it will cost less than £500 to fix and the parts will be here in a few days.' Express news accurately and indicate that matters could have been worse, or that the result will be advantageous to the customer.

Accountants, architects, consultants, doctors, lawyers

Reality check Arrange short review meetings early in the project to ensure that expectations are aligned with likely outcomes. Perceptions are crucial, so it is important to check that everything is going to plan in the mind of the client.

Time expectations Setting time expectations is important, especially where outside agencies or external factors may cause delays. For example, an architect applying for planning permission on behalf of a client needs to factor in the time it could take to get a decision from a planning office. Best- and worst-case scenarios sometimes prevent disappointment. Different clients take in meaning in different forms. Therefore communicate timescales using both words and illustrative diagrams or flow charts.

Bad news early Avoid or manage surprises. When you have bad news, it should be given as soon as possible. However, ensure you allow some short internal thinking time in order to develop and offer solutions to mitigate the effect of the bad news. In particular be prepared to help your client contacts explain the new situation to their superiors. Give them the right words, phrases or reassurances to pass up the line.

Making customers feel important – something individual

Mary Kay Ash, the Texan entrepreneur who built up the American cosmetic empire, wrote in her biography, *The Mary Kay Way* (2008), her precept: 'Whenever I meet someone, I try to imagine him or her wearing an invisible sign that says: make me feel important! I respond to this sign immediately, and it works wonders.' Every one of us is an individual. We have our own personal characteristics, unique fingerprints and unique DNA. Our individuality is important to us and we believe that we are somehow special.

It is all relative

Feeling more favoured than others makes people happy. This has become clear from research into happiness. Studies in the USA by Firebaugh and Tach (2005) indicate that after physical health, *relative* income is the most important determinant of happiness. Firebaugh of Pennsylvania State University argues that, in evaluating their own incomes, individuals naturally compare themselves to their peers of the same age. The richer you are relative to your age peers, the happier you tend to be. Positive impressions emerge when individuals calibrate themselves against their peer group and find themselves better off. Carrying this logic through to service situations, positive impressions will result where we are able to make each customer feel more favoured, relative to others. If we can make customers feel important, we can lift perceptions further as in Figure A5.1.

> if we can make customers feels important, we can lift perceptions further

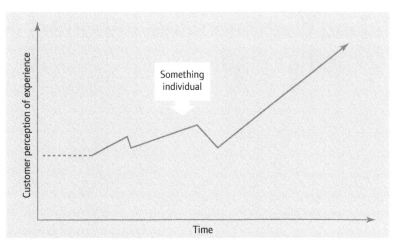

FIGURE A5.1 Satisfaction curve – something individual

Avoid making customers feel unimportant

The corollary is certainly true: making customers feel *unimportant* results in negative perceptions. See the difference in these two experiences:

In the first coffee shop, at a busy time, a shopper places her order, pays and takes a seat. When the coffee order is complete a server walks around the restaurant calling 'medium latte', expecting her to identify herself. Her identity has not been remembered. Picture the contrast in the second coffee shop. When she orders her coffee, the barista takes her name and writes it on the cup, so it can be offered to her by name. As another option, a customer could be given a flag with a number or a symbol on it to stand on their table, so that the server can find them immediately. Treating people indifferently can leave customers feeling unimportant.

Keeping customers waiting needlessly or treating them unfairly can result in the mood of the customer slipping downwards. For instance, if they see another buyer dealt with ahead of them or given conspicuously more favourable attention, this can be resented. If there will be reasons for one customer to 'jump the queue', it is better to pre-warn other customers, or at least justify this as it happens. We have seen how hospital accident and emergency receptions place a sign advising, 'Patients are seen in order of clinical need' so that first arrivals with minor injuries can expect serious emergencies to be seen before them.

Important customers are happier customers

Customers who are made to feel important are easier to serve, respond better to serving staff and return to buy more. Most critically of all, they have a personal reason to recommend your business to others. Figure A5.2 shows the contrasting emotions.

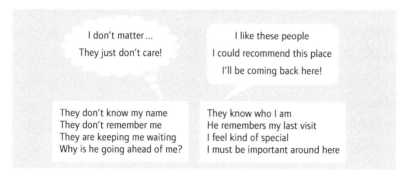

FIGURE A5.2 Unimportant or important?

So how can you make customers feel important?

Ten techniques to make customers feel important

1 Use the customer's name and title

A customer's name is their most precious possession. Research shows that if a person has two streams of dialogue presented to them simultaneously via two headphones, they tune in to the voice that has used their name. Using a customer's name several times during the encounter (though not slavishly) is a sign of respect and recognition. Recently in Buenos Aires, I slotted my Bank Card into a cash machine outside an Argentine bank. On entering my PIN number a message appeared on the screen: 'Welcome Mr Cram'. I was surprised and delighted because my own bank at home does not do this. They have the information but do not use it.

Customers whose names are difficult to pronounce will appreciate the effort even more – since it is likely to be a rare experience for them. It is normally better to attempt the pronunciation and ask if this is correct – it demonstrates that you aim to succeed. Then use the name correctly later in the transaction to reveal that you have remembered it. Beyond the name, many customers have a preferred salutation – for example, *Doctor* or *Professor* – that you can use during the conversation. If a customer has a particular title, it is respectful to use it – the famous actor Sir Michael Caine reportedly refuses to open an envelope unless it is correctly addressed:

> *I refuse to open any mail that does not say* Sir Michael *on it. If they don't put* Sir *on the envelope, they don't know anything about me, so why should I open the letter?*

Sir Michael Caine

How to do it Use systems to ensure that names are checked and entered accurately into any database at the outset. Right first time is far simpler than any subsequent correction. Make it easy for customers to rectify any error.

Try to discover and record the preferred name. Anthony is the name on my passport, so airlines call me Anthony when I board, though like many people I prefer the abbreviated form of my name. Trailfinders, the tailor-made travel company, has an automatic number recognition system, so when a regular customer calls, the agent answering is able to use their preferred name during the conversation.

try to discover and record the preferred name

Where a name is visible on a payment card or correspondence, use it. Even if the customer can see you reading it out, they still appreciate the implication that you care enough to personalise for them. It is straightforward to call men by the title: 'Mr'. For women, the neutral 'Ms' is less judgemental unless you know that they prefer the title 'Miss' or 'Mrs'. Some establishments have chosen to use '*Madame*' for ladies over the age of 25 (following the French style of greeting married and unmarried women over this age).

Encourage and acknowledge human memory. Praise staff members who make the effort to remember the names of repeat customers. Teach people simple memory techniques to recall names. Rehearse the use of names in service training sessions. Mystery shoppers can monitor how often and how effectively this approach is used in practice.

2 Show you are listening carefully

If you make it evident that you are attending to what the customer says, they will feel more valued. You are demonstrating that their information or briefing is important. This applies to a professional brief to a lawyer, a check-in for an airline or the quick handover of a car for a routine service.

How to do it The best way to convince a customer you are listening carefully is to be genuinely interested in what they are saying. Sincerity shows. To reinforce this, there are specific techniques such as repeating the exact words the customer has emphasised, paraphrasing to demonstrate understanding and pausing to confirm the customer's wishes. Interrupting the customer may imply that the agent feels what is being said is unimportant. Avoid speaking very much more rapidly than the customer. If agents speak very quickly it carries the implication that they are trying to speed customers through the process in a standard manner. Build rapport by matching the speed of speech to the pace of the customer. Talking too quickly or too slowly for a given customer may be interpreted as disrespectful, so balance your word delivery against their benchmark. If they act seriously, respond in a professional manner. If they behave informally, moderate your style slightly, to put them at their ease.

> build rapport by matching the speed of speech to the pace of the customer

Social media can also be used to demonstrate that a brand is attentive to its customers. Harvester Restaurants use Facebook to show customers that they are listening carefully. Diners can connect with Harvester through Facebook and log their comments on the food or the dining experience. Harvester responds quickly to thank customers for praise and to address instances of criticism.

3 Eye contact

Making eye contact with a customer in a face-to-face encounter is important. Without this, some important connection has been missed.

How to do it In professional services and service shops the eye contact happens naturally, but it can lapse in high-volume mass service. For example, bank tellers can serve a stream of customers with no eye contact. A neat solution used by some banks is to place on the teller's screen a tickbox section to confirm the customer's eye colour. This requires the teller to look at the customer's eyes to answer.

4 Appreciation

People feel more important when their own contribution is recognised and appreciated. Therefore you should notice and thank customers for small actions they have taken to make the service easier to provide. For example, 'thanks for having your account number ready'.

How to do it The words 'thank you' are often used in a standard fashion at the start of a service encounter – 'thank you for calling us today' – or right at the end of the transaction – 'thank you for your business'. These forms of thank you are often taken for granted by customers, simply because they are part of the expected routine and are only noted when omitted. More impact can be created when thanks are given in mid-transaction for something specific. You can review a sample of transactions, say 20 or 30, and identify a range of actions taken by customers to make life easy for the serving staff. Then highlight these to servers and encourage them to pause and make a very brief comment of thanks for future customers who take these actions. The outcome should be small signs of appreciation to make customers feel good during the encounter.

5 Praise in public, reprimand privately

Everyone feels important when praised and feels unimportant when corrected. This universality is magnified when it is carried out in front of others.

How to do it If you are serving your customers in public or working with a group of clients or a team of buyers, seek opportunities to highlight anything that reflects well on them. Look for 'the best', 'the first', 'the highest', 'the fastest' and draw attention to it. The message to the audience should be to reflect credit and reinforce the eminence of this particular customer. Conversely, when a client working in a group makes an error, take great care to inform the individual discretely and on their own. Any apparent public humiliation will be long remembered.

6 Recall a previous encounter

A vivid example is recounted in the book *Living Service* by Marc Silvester and Mohi Ahmed (2008), where a colleague left an expensive fountain pen in her hotel room in Chicago. Checking into the same hotel two years' later the receptionist handed her the pen. There had been no forwarding address, but the hotel had retained the pen against her name in case she returned.

Recalling something of the previous conversation can impress a customer markedly. When a customer rang to enquire about a trip to China, the Trailfinders agent had the details of previous trips on screen and was able to ask – how was the visit to Panama? The waitress, Charlie, in Graffiti restaurant in Harpenden remembered a couple six months after their previous visit, and asked 'Do you want the same as last time?' And during the meal, she also remembered the original desserts.

How to do it Create systems to permit customer-facing staff to record individual notes by customer. The telesales staff of a UK brewery recorded the due date for a pub landlord's goat to give birth to kids, so that they could show interest in a matter important to him.

Capture information early in the encounter and share it with other team-members. The hall porter at the Ritz-Carlton in Singapore helps guests by taking luggage from their taxi. As he does so, he asks if they have stayed before. If the answer is yes, he tugs his left ear in sight of the receptionist, who is able to say 'Welcome back'.

Judgement is necessary where the customer has confided something more personal to the person serving them. In this instance, it is best not to pass this on to other staff in case the customer feels a breach of confidence has taken place. However, if the same person is serving the customer, the recollection of something confided creates a closer feeling of rapport.

Role play with staff to rehearse bringing relevant information into conversation as naturally as possible. Sometimes it is safer to refer to the previous occasion as a question rather than a statement. In any event it should come over positively and in context.

7 Remembering tastes without being asked

Guests at Marriott hotels find their requirements recognised without needing to repeat them at check-in. The Marriott Automated Reservation System for Hotel Accommodation (Marsha) database records preferences of regular guests such as liking a room on a lower floor or close to the elevator. It simply happens each time they stay. No drama, no need for a reminder.

The client executive of an advertising agency brings the 'normal' coffee, tea or sparkling mineral water when clients arrive, showing that they have remembered the tastes of the individuals concerned. This will be implemented without comment unless the circumstances differ. For instance, on a very warm day, the client may be asked, 'Your normal black coffee, or would you prefer iced water?'

How to do it Research and identify aspects of service requirements that are likely to remain consistent for a particular customer, but differ between customers. Test in practice that customers do indeed appreciate this quiet form of recognition.

Capture the necessary information and validate after a period if necessary.

Train staff to follow through with considerate actions that incorporate this customer insight.

> train staff to follow through with considerate actions

8 Senior contact

When a celebrity arrives at a restaurant the head chef will often meet, greet and seat them himself, to acknowledge their importance. Using a senior person to make customers feel special is a technique that is effective and memorable. To celebrate the airline's tenth anniversary in November 2005, easyJet founder, Stelios Haji-Ioannou, greeted passengers on the mid-morning flight with champagne. They will recall this flight with the top man for many years.

When a customer anniversary is achieved such as five years of buying or a grand total of tonnage hitting a magic number, the recognition from a senior executive can make a customer feel truly valued. In professional services businesses, the small account may value the occasional special attention of senior management more than the major account.

How to do it There are twin concepts behind this action. From the customer's viewpoint the senior executive is showing that the customer is valued. From the company perspective, the executive is playing a dual role: partly a representative of management and partly another member of the customer relations team. This latter role requires that the executive be briefed beforehand to be able to show knowledge and awareness of the customer and to ask appropriate questions. A good brief will vary according to the type of business, but may well include some of the following: customer name, location, purchased products and value, length of time as a customer, significant landmarks in the relationship, complaints or issues that have arisen in the past, current concerns, opportunities for business in the future, questions to ask.

A short review may take place after the meeting to establish any issues and opportunities that have emerged.

9 Preferential treatment

In all businesses there are examples where priority must be given for urgent needs. Car manufacturers prioritise parts deliveries where a vehicle is otherwise off the road. Hospitals prioritise patients most at risk. Alongside meeting urgent needs, businesses can choose to give priority to specific customers as recognition of their importance. It may be preference in time, location or personnel. For example, in an airport, business-class passengers often receive fast-track service to save time and the inconvenience of waiting in a slow security queue. Reserving the best tables for the most loyal customers is common practice in restaurants. Ensuring that the most qualified professionals serve the highest priority accounts is a strategy in professional services firms.

Of course, some customers will be more valuable than others. Airlines make more money from business-class passengers than the economy travellers, yet why make the economy passengers walk through business-class seating to reach their seats? This seems like drawing attention to their lesser status and it may be smarter to separate different priority categories of customers.

How to do it The first requirement is to identify your most valuable customers. This may be as simple as a ranking by turnover or tonnage. Best practice goes further and looks at customer profitability and other values to the firm. For example, a division of a large Swedish paper company scores customers on a weighted scale including volume, profitability, scope for business growth, openness to share strategy, value as a source of new business ideas.

Secondly, the potential areas for prioritisation are listed. In a business to business relationship, examples could include: privileged access to information, advance warnings of changes, access to key people, production preference, additional customisation, more flexible warranties and enhanced service and technical support, entertainment programmes.

Thirdly, the customers and benefits are matched, so that customers receive a level of priority according to their value and that their particular benefits are relevant to their needs and interests.

Finally, measures of customer satisfaction can calibrate the effectiveness of this approach.

10 Giving customers power to help others

A firm can make its customers feel important by extending to them the ability to help and support others. For example, the car insurance company Direct Line allows named drivers to build up a no-claims bonus while driving on the policy of the car-owner.

This allows parents to help their children achieve lower-cost insurance policies when they come to insure their own vehicles. Shoppers at Waitrose food stores are given a green token as they leave the checkout. They can choose between three containers to place their token, with each container representing a different local charity. At the end of the month, Waitrose donates £1000 among the three charities according to the proportion of tokens in the containers. Customers are given the power to help others through the charitable donations of a company they buy from.

How to do it Investigate the motivations and concerns of customers. The results can be used creatively. For example, Proctor & Gamble uncovered an insight in their research studying the motivations of mothers buying Pampers diapers. The insight was a bond between new mothers that led to a desire to help mothers less fortunate than themselves. Proctor & Gamble began a link with UNICEF in the UK in 2006 – extended to USA and other countries in October 2008 – to work towards eliminating Maternal and Newborn Tetanus by 2012. The 'One pack = One vaccine' campaign resulted in 50 million vaccines in its first two years and is expected to fund 200 million more vaccines by 2012. Potentially saving another baby's life with a purchase can make a mother feel especially important. The way such research is put into practice requires sensitivity and credibility. In a world that is often cynical, good partners and long-term commitments are essential to convince customers in this emotional area.

UNICEF was also the partner of choice for the phone company Orange, who understood that their customers wanted a quick and easy way to donate to disaster relief funds. Soon after the 2010 earthquake in Haiti, Orange sent a text explaining how UK subscribers could authorise a £2.50 donation to the Haiti Children's fund from their phone accounts. Customers moved by the heart-rending news reports were able to respond with a donation rapidly and conveniently.

Helping others may have even more power in challenging times. In 2007, Ritz-Carlton identified that some corporate event planners were concerned about the appropriateness of expensive company meetings at high-end locations. Ritz-Carlton announced 'Meaningful Meetings'. Subject to a minimum of ten bed-nights, the company will donate 10% of the corporate meeting fee split between the organiser's choice of charity and the Ritz-Carlton foundation 'Community Footprints'.

A process for finding ways to make customers feel important

There are many ways of making customers feel important. The Canadian service thinker Paul Levesque adds an insightful element in his book, *Customer Service from the Inside Out Made Easy* (2006). He provides a structured approach, segmenting the service encounter into sequential steps in a process, so that you can enhance the customer's experience and sentiments at each step (Figure A5.3). His special insight is the sixth and final step in his process – make sure the customer notices what you are doing for him or her!

> make sure the customer notices what are you doing for him or her!

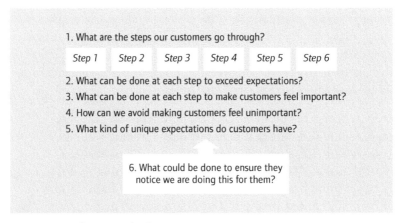

FIGURE A5.3 Levesque's six steps

Paul Levesque's steps help service providers build a more individual outcome for customers:

1 **What are the various steps our customers typically go through as a part of this particular transaction?** With the service team, list the stages and sequence of actions to serve customers.

2 **What could be done in each step of the transaction sequence to exceed our customers' expectations?** Move into a creative session with the customer service team to generate initial ideas.

3 **What could be done in each step of the transaction process to make our customers feel important?** After the first creative burst has subsided, ask this question to add further ideas.

4 **Is there anything we could stop doing in each step to avoid customers feeling unimportant?** Use this question to explore the converse of question 3.

5 **What kinds of unique expectations do customers of particular categories have when they do business with us?** Take this angle to find new ways to customise.

6 **What could be done to ensure that this particular category of customer knows we are doing this with them in mind?** Finally, look for touches, words and actions that draw good service to the customer's attention. Make sure they note that it is being done for them.

To receive the commercial benefit for excellent service, providers must ensure that customers notice the tailoring and personalisation done for them. For this reason, feedback is valuable. Ask customers which elements they noted, what they appreciated. Check what buyers value by surveying a representative sample of customers immediately after the service experience. Survey another sample the following day to see what is recalled – this is likely to be the message passed on to friends and colleagues.

Your research can teach you how to ensure that your customer consideration is recognised. What are the phrases or gestures that carry the greatest effect? For example, customer feedback in one business demonstrated that clients remembered and liked the phrase 'for quick reference' when the switchboard took a phone message and said, 'May I take your phone number for quick reference?' The phrase implies that the person will want to ring them as soon as they get the message and that the customer is important to them. You could also identify phrases that irritate that you can remove from scripts and dialogues.

Making the customer feel important is a simple secret of success.

HOW TO APPLY

Something individual: making customers feel important

APPLICATION: MASS SERVICE

Airlines, banks, hotels, logistics, retailing, train-operating companies

Active listening Listening carefully shows customers that you are treating them as important, especially if it is a special purchase or an unusual transaction. Listening to an order and writing it down or entering it into the system in the customer's sight is reassuring. It can be helpful to confirm back to the customer exactly what has been heard. Do it right *and* show the customer it has been done right.

Recognition and use of customers' names Airlines can make passengers feel important by using their names during the journey. Security requirements within air travel mean that the names of passengers are known. An exception is someone who is already important – some senior company executives and celebrities who may seek anonymity. On this subject, dates of birth will be visible on passports and in the databases of frequent flier programmes. However, one unassuming executive travelling on his birthday was embarrassed to be given birthday greetings at every point in his journey, including a spontaneous singing of 'Happy Birthday' by fellow passengers when the pilot announced it over the intercom. Once is enough!

In the context of train travel, names are less likely to be known, but where, for example, credit cards are used then it is possible to thank people by name.

Hotels will see guest names at check-in, checkout and in restaurants. In other places use of names will depend on staff memory. Some Marriott hotels retain photographs of important regular guests and encourage associates (staff members) to greet them by name.

Bank tellers and phone-banking agents can use the customer's name during the transaction because they will have the information in front of them. A good information system will include preferred form of address. Nationwide and Virgin Money agents simply ask 'Is it OK to call you by your first name?' Likewise when a credit card is presented the name is visible and it should be used.

Offering choices Travellers and guests may feel that they are under the control of cabin or train crew/hotel staff and this can diminish their sense of importance. One method of counteracting this is by offering choices and options whenever practicable. Making decisions – even small ones – gives back a sense of authority.

Thanking customers During a complex transaction with a retailer or a bank, there may be a need for information or guidance from the customer. Such help should be acknowledged and a brief thank-you given. Everyone likes to be thanked.

Extending the retail encounter Customers who feel important are likely to linger longer or be open to further transactions. The longer customers remain in a department store or a bookshop, for example, the more they are likely to spend. So make the retail customer feel important and they will stay longer. When a bank customer is made to feel that he matters to the bank and has a successful phone transaction, he is more open to a cross-selling initiative. Do not mandate every agent to end each incoming call robotically with a plea to buy insurance this month. Instead, it is smarter to identify the next likely product for every customer and only make the suggestion if the caller has responded warmly during the call. The warm response comes when the customer feels important.

Preferential treatment Airlines and hotels are leaders in providing systematic preferential treatment via frequent flier/guest databases. They use incentives like upgrades, free flights and free nights to reward regular customers, such that flier points have even been featured in divorce settlements. Train-operating companies are now recording the names of first-class season ticket holders to provide them with the benefits of convenience and privileges.

Helping others Aer Lingus, Alitalia, All Nippon Airways (ANA), American Airlines, Asiana Airlines, British Airways, Cathay Pacific, Finnair, JAL and QANTAS participate in the Change for Good® programme with UNICEF, which enables travellers to hand in their foreign currency to raise funds for needy children in 150 countries around the world.

Hospitals, car repairers, travel agents

Use of names and recognition Hospitals, car repairers and travel agents are well placed to know and use the names of patients and customers. Thus personalisation should follow naturally, so much so that its absence will be noted. Furthermore, they should keep records of preferred names and be prepared for surprises. A bright young nurse read a patient's surname on the bed-head chart and enthusiastically asked the patient for her first name, assuming she would like this intimacy. The surly answer came back 'Mrs!' The older lady wanted to preserve her dignity – the only person who called her 'Doris' was her husband.

These enterprises are able to show recognition because they will have accurate records of previous visits, treatments or repairs. Positive references can be made to these previous occasions and this will enhance feelings of importance.

Avoiding the unimportance trap Where records are kept, customers/patients will resent being asked the same questions twice because it implies that the organisation cannot be troubled to look up the record. Instead, phrase the question as a need to confirm that records are still correct.

Where possible, hospitals should seek ways to offer choices so that patients have some feeling of control over parts of their stay. They will feel more involved and therefore more important. Likewise car owners can feel helpless when their car is defective and appreciate choices or options in the solution.

All these types of enterprises should avoid very small print (below 10 point) for letters and reports and documents, as older people will have difficulty in reading them and will feel excluded. Remember they may feel embarrassed to highlight their declining vision and be reluctant to ask for help – especially men!

Patient consideration Help young, fit and healthy hospital nurses to empathise with the awkwardness and difficulties faced by a geriatric patient or someone with a hand in plaster. A useful exercise is to place a breakfast tray in front of them and invite them to butter toast and eat a boiled egg one-handed … using their non-dominant hand! It is a memorable reminder!

Treating people with dignity Car owners, patients and irregular travellers will be aware of the limits to their expertise. They deserve consideration in hearing things explained in layman's terms without jargon and specialist vocabulary. Give appropriate information in a timely and sensitive way. All hospitals are aware of the special requirements of privacy and dignity of patients. However not all hospitals are using best practices to ensure that patients *notice* that they are respecting their privacy and dignity.

Care and concern for others In the medical world, there is another significant constituency – carers. They may be family or friends. Giving them credit for the good work and the effectiveness of their support pays dividends in encouraging their continuing support and also leads to positive word-of-mouth endorsements.

Accountants, architects, consultants, doctors, lawyers

Recognise the value of their input Laymen approaching an accountant, auditor, architect, surveyor or lawyer will be aware of the qualifications and expertise held by the professional. An overly authoritative style may risk diminishing the client's feeling of importance. Clearly the professional must show his or her expertise, and at the same time make the client feel their abilities are recognised:

▌ Praise clients for the clarity of a brief

▌ Remark on the comprehensiveness of answers

▌ Recognise when they ask good questions

▌ Thank them for the preparation they have put in

Make them smarter clients Teach your clients skills that they lacked before. Offer seminars. Encourage them to recognise that they learn more with every meeting or encounter. Guide them in gathering and presenting information. Teach them how to construct a case. This will make them feel more effective, and in return they will be easier clients to work with in the future. Educate them about the niceties of tax law. Surprise them with unusual applications of principles. If they learn interesting facts, angles or skills then they will be proud to discuss these with family, friends and colleagues, leading to an endorsement for your practice.

Help your client shine in their organisation A client who gains recognition or promotion in their own organisation through support from you is a real asset. Can you help them to be more important in their company? Providing them with information that will impress their boss. Thought leadership is designed to make your client look up-to-speed in challenging areas. Give rapid updates. Deliver project summaries that show their contribution. Explain the meaning of legislation that may impact on them. Above all give them actionable advice that helps them get results. Be an advocate for your customers. Find ways to communicate their successes in their industry.

I can fix that – service recovery

The words 'I can fix that' came second in a consumer survey in the USA for the most beautiful words you can hear – beaten by the number one favourite word, hearing the sound of your own name! Fixing problems is a highly rated virtue.

Most customers have experienced poor responses to service shortfalls. They rate a convincing recovery very highly. Of course every company aims to deliver an error-free service experience. Yet in practice, even among the best service brands, the results can fall short. In fact academics have argued that services have unique characteristics to make it impossible to ensure 100% error-free service. One characteristic is that the customer co-produces the experience with the provider; hence a customer may provide incorrect initial information or misunderstand instructions. Another characteristic is that a service is being produced at the same time as the client is receiving it. It is too late to inspect or check afterwards. For manifold reasons, errors will occur. Act 6 is about setting matters right with style and confidence – defining a world-class recovery, as in Figure A6.1.

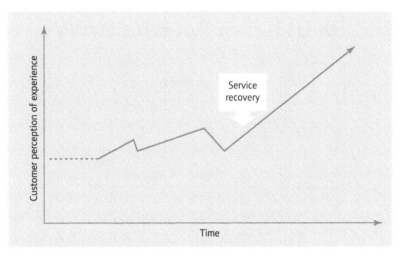

FIGURE A6.1 Satisfaction curve – service recovery

The recovery may be an answer to a company mistake. Or the customer may have been at fault. For example, I dropped my passport on the floor of an Arlanda Express as I jumped out at Stockholm airport. My gratitude was huge when it was returned to me by the train manager. She had scanned the photograph inside and recognised me running back in panic. Either way, when a problem arises, your objective is to prove your responsiveness and effectiveness. You want customers to say: 'You can rely on them – and if *ever* something does go wrong, they fix it for me fast. I'd recommend them to anyone.'

Customer perception counts

Furthermore, customer perceptions count for more than technical reality. If the customer feels that there is a problem or they feel disappointed, then you have a recovery opportunity. It doesn't matter that the service was performed correctly to normal operating standards. It doesn't matter that external factors caused a problem. It doesn't matter that the customer caused the problem by carelessness or created their own unrealistic expectations. Whatever the starting point, manage the customer's emotional journey through the encounter to end the experience on a high note.

> manage the customer's emotional journey through the encounter to end the experience on a high note

A problem … or an opportunity?

There is a belief that a customer who experiences a failure, followed by a brilliant service recovery, may rate their satisfaction higher than if no problem had arisen. This is known as the *service paradox,* as illustrated in Figure A6.2. Imagine one traveller, having heard stories of late-arriving flights, who rates his satisfaction with the airline's service at the lower end of the scale despite an on-time arrival. Another traveller, whose flight is delayed, is delighted with the immediate care and concern she received from airline staff speeding her through the airport to catch her flight connection. She gives the airline a high rating for service.

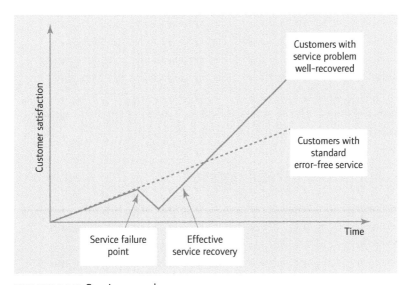

FIGURE A6.2 Service paradox

Academic service researchers are divided on the validity of the service paradox. Hart, Heskett and Sasser (1990) state that 'a good recovery can turn angry frustrated customers into loyal ones. It can in fact create more goodwill than if things had gone smoothly in the first place.' In contrast, McCollough, Berry and Yadav (2000) found in their research that 'excellent recovery is not an opportunity when compared to the satisfaction resulting from error-free service delivery'.

Of 15 studies conducted into the service paradox between 1992 and 2007, seven confirm its validity. Eight others refute the paradox, concluding that the best way to please customers is with a reliable first-time error-free delivery. According to these findings a service recovery strategy is simply a means to limit the harm from the failure, not an opportunity to impress the customer.

The jury is out: the service paradox may or may not exist. However, all researchers agree that first-time error-free service is preferable, more cost-effective and likely to lead to loyalty and positive referral. In addition there is agreement that when a failure occurs, a strong service recovery is the correct strategy. A poor recovery is seen as 'double deviation' with a second disappointment on top of the original shortfall. In some circumstances a strong recovery may simply approach the status quo. In other circumstances the recovery may be beneficial in restoring satisfaction and achieving delight in the recovery process. Strong recoveries go some way to restoring trust in the supplier and encourage repurchase. The creative aspect of the recovery may also inspire customers to give positive word-of-mouth reports among their peers.

An opportunity to be noticed

A recovery can achieve a moment of attention in a routine business. Who notices the on-time train, or the phone call that comes through or the delivery that arrives when expected? The consequence of good service is that it is simply taken for granted.

On the other hand, extraordinary efforts to fix a problem will be noticed. Christmas gifts should arrive in time, and it seemed good news for Canadian Michel Cuhaci when he received the parcel from Amazon containing the physics textbook *A Student's Guide to Maxwell's Equations*. It was to be a gift to his nephew studying electromagnetics. The parcel from Amazon arrived on 24 December

2008. Sadly, when he skimmed the book, he discovered that the first 38 pages were missing. He immediately posted a complaint message on the Amazon website, giving the book a one-star review. The author, Professor Dan Fleisch, saw the review and decided that the only response was to promise a replacement copy of the book. It was Christmas Eve, however. No courier could provide an immediate delivery. To keep the promise the Professor took the 6 a.m. flight on Christmas morning from Ohio to Ottawa and rented a car to hand-deliver the replacement book to Michel Cuhaci's home. The one-star review has been modified:

> *My rating of 1 star (based on the first book I received, since I could not read the full content of the misprinted issue) now could be changed to 5 star. However, if I change it to 5 star, most review readers could miss the 'happy ending' (read follow-up comments), and the Author's concern and excellent service on a winter stormy day ...*

> **www.amazon.com/Students-Guide-Maxwells-Equations/**
> **product-reviews/0521701473**

A huge number of people have read this review. Few physics textbooks have ever attracted as many reviews and comments on Amazon as this one!

Attention and emotion = memory

When something goes wrong in service delivery, you have the full and undivided attention of the customer. The failure is a challenge to accepted pattern. Expect your customers to be more sensitised than normal. They may be upset or angry with the company who has let them down. They may be fearful for the consequences. They may be puzzled and blaming themselves. Customers go through deep emotions when services fail. Emotional experiences lay down deep memories. Research by Talarico, Labar and Rubin (2004), first presented to the American Psychological Society in 2003, demonstrates that the *intensity* of the experience explains the variation in autobiographical memory, to a far greater degree than the recency of the experience or whether the experience was positive or negative. Good and bad events stay with us for the duration. You recall vividly the high days and the low days, but a thousand other days fade into a blur of ordinariness, shown in Figure A6.3.

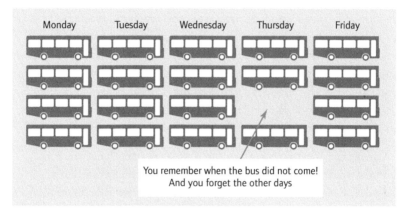

FIGURE A6.3 Remembering service failure

This means that your response to the service failure is likely to be remembered. Treat the recovery process as if you are on camera, because the 'memory camera' is running in your customer's head. For some types of service, you may have other customers witnessing the event and the recall impact is magnified. It is important to turn the error (or perceived shortfall) to your advantage.

Empowerment

The time window for recovery from many service errors is small. A service is being produced at the same time as the customer is receiving it. The time for fixing a problem is when it arises. If a service error is not corrected quickly – especially for high-cost services – it becomes nearly impossible to regain the level of customer trust. This requires the empowerment of the service staff. They need the authority and power to say, 'I can fix that'.

Fixing problems fast can improve the customer experience and save money. First Direct resolve 75% of complaints within 24 hours and claim that speedy recovery reduces compensation costs. Shaw and Ivens (2002) quote David Mead, then First Direct chief operating officer who launched the service recovery principles that he called 'No Mess'. He said, 'We empowered the representatives dealing with complaints to decide there and then whether some monetary compensation was appropriate.' This approach was a demonstration of trust in his representatives. Naturally there was a management concern that this might increase the costs of recovery. Mead responded, 'In fact they've come down! The reason is that people are solving complaints and issues much earlier, before they get out of control.' In practice, the longer a complaint remains unaddressed the more compensation an annoyed customer will demand.

Empowering the learning process

Empowered representatives will solve new problems or find better responses. Every day a new situation comes about. Customers change. Other customer service providers create higher standards. New technologies come available. Every customer service glitch, every complaint or concern, is a chance to learn. Learning must be captured and disseminated.

The best practice is to hold regular reviews of problems, recovery situations, responses and results:

▌ When did the problem first become evident?

▌ How did the customer express the problem?

▌ What phrases did they use?

▌ What facts were quoted?

▌ What emotion was conveyed?

▌ What did the customer expect?

▌ What options were discussed?

▌ What explanation was given?

▌ How did the customer respond to this?

▌ What was the agreement?

▌ How did the encounter close?

▌ What would you have done differently?

Difficult cases can inspire representatives to generate new and creative responses. Role play is an effective tool. The representative who faced the customer plays the role of the customer in re-enacting the situation. Other staff members role play alternative reactions, so that the best possible process and outcome are achieved.

Angry is dangerous

A key lesson from such reviews is that anger is a barrier to moving on. Service disruption can be annoying and some customers are quick to anger when they feel they are neglected, served badly or treated without respect. However, you cannot educate or inform an angry customer. Anger is destructive. Angry customers upset staff, annoy or alarm other customers, damage equipment, and even injure themselves. It is important to calm them quickly. Only then can you begin to resolve matters.

There are many ways to defuse anger. The simplest approaches are the best. Listen and remain calm. Do not take it personally. If the customer says, 'What kind of shoddy company is this?' he is venting his emotions rather than criticising you as an individual. At the first opportunity to speak without interrupting – perhaps when the customer is taking a breath for the next tirade – come in with something positive like 'Let's see how we can fix this' or 'Please give me a chance to put things right'. It is important to avoid any rebuttal or defensive response that the customer will take as further provocation. Use a phrase like 'It certainly sounds like something has gone wrong here – let's take a look at the next step.'

> avoid any rebuttal or defensive response that the customer will take as further provocation

Angry letters and emails should wherever possible receive a telephone response. Oral communication is better suited to conveying compassion and empathy to irate customers, than written communication. An answering letter or email may address the service problem, but not soothe the emotional aspect. Even an attempt to make phone contact can smooth the path, so that the letter can begin with 'I tried to speak to you on the phone to resolve this ...'. The aim is to diffuse the anger so that a solution can be applied.

Call centres are often a target for anger, especially when a problem is compounded by a long wait to be answered. If the customer becomes abusive and uses bad language, it is proper to give a firm warning that this is unacceptable. There are phrases that can be used to bring customers back in line. The agent may say, 'I am forbidden to continue a call when threats or bad language are being used. Let's say that I did not hear what you said then, but if you repeat it, then I would have to end this call.'

Sometimes the angry customer will calm down if the first agent asks for agreement to transfer the call to a supervisor, or an experienced colleague. The implied escalation and the new voice can bring the customer back to a calmer mood.

Once the customer is calm, you are ready to begin the recovery process.

What is a world-class recovery?

Diners choose expensive restaurants for excellent food and great service. Charlie Trotter says that guests 'expect perfection, or whatever their definition of it is' (Lawler, 2001). Inevitably, delivery will sometimes inevitably fall short of expectations. In his view, the difference between a good restaurant and a great one is how they correct a mistake and learn from it. According to the restaurant's unwritten rules of recovery, the first step calls for an honest and sincere apology. The next step is to resolve the problem. The list below shows the stages in a world-class recovery:

1. Listen carefully.
2. Take ownership of the situation.
3. Show empathy.
4. Consider the individual.
5. Offer a choice of solutions.
6. Demonstrate fairness.
7. Keep the new promise.
8. Learn from the event.

1 Listen carefully

Invite the customer to explain. Thank the customer for drawing the issue to your attention. Show you are listening by repeating a key piece of information, asking questions and checking that you have understood correctly. Writing notes is another indicator that you are taking notice. Your aim is two-fold. You are demonstrating respect to the customer through treating their issue seriously. You are also working to identify the problem and define the bottom-line issue.

2 Take ownership of the situation

Apologise for the situation arising and show that you are responsible for bringing about a resolution. The first part is recognising and apologising for the customer's inconvenience, which is not the same as acknowledging any wrongdoing. Avoid placing blame on the customer – asking if they understood the ordering procedure may ignite the anger again. Avoid placing blame on your company unless it is obviously at fault.

The second part is identifying yourself as owning the problem. Every employee of Ritz-Carlton Hotels carries a card in their wallet to remind them of the 20 'Basics' of their business. Statement eight reads: 'Any employee who receives a complaint, owns the complaint.' If the complaint resolution requires a transfer to another person, then the customer should be aware that the first person has handed on a full briefing and the second person should identify themselves as accountable. Just as in a relay race, the baton should not be dropped.

3 Show empathy

This means creating rapport by aligning with the customer. Showing empathy is about engaging with a customer who is feeling aggrieved or unhappy. You may need to show empathy to move the customer towards a resolution. There is a well-proven and non-threatening three-step formula to help customers consider another viewpoint. It is known as the '3 Fs' or 'feel, felt, found':

> *What kind of appalling service is this?? Totally*
> *unacceptable!!*

*I understand how you feel ... Other customers have felt
exactly the same way ... They have found that ...*

Step 1: 'Feel' The customer has explained the problem and is
looking to you to react. Your opening sentence
should include the word 'feel'. This develops
harmony. Immediately you recognise their
feelings and show that you are taking their
emotions seriously. It invites them to listen
further without interrupting. For example,
you say, 'I am sorry you feel this way' or 'I can
understand how you feel' or 'I know why you
feel frustrated'.

Step 2: 'Felt' You move on to express empathy directly and
imply that they are being reasonable and are
not alone. They belong to a group of people
who have felt this way. You draw on historical
perspective and indicate that this is part of
a bigger picture. This moves the customer to
recognise your experience in dealing with
similar situations. You say, 'Other customers
have felt the same way' or 'I would have felt as
surprised as you are before I worked here' or 'A
customer yesterday felt exactly as you do'.

Step 3: 'Found' Having built harmony and gained recognition
for your experience, you convert this
experience into a conclusion. Findings carry
the association of deep knowledge or research
and represent a solution or an answer. The
word 'found' implies discovery of something
worthwhile. This moves the customer to take
your recommendation seriously. You say, 'What
I found was that I needed to allow extra time',
or 'These customers found that our guarantee
was more generous than other suppliers'.

An example of the 3 Fs in use appears in Heppel's book *Five
Star Service* (2005). He recommends an answer to the customer

complaining that they have called three times with the same kind of problem and had to explain it to a new person each time. The response runs as follows:

> *I understand that you must feel frustrated with this. If I had explained the problem three times, I am sure I would have felt the same. I've found that if I hear the details directly from our customer, I am able to understand the issues more clearly and resolve the problem more rapidly, rather than reading some notes from a computer screen.*

Heppel, 2005, p. 50

The 3 Fs approach works well when the examples you are citing are genuine and credible.

4 Consider the individual

Recovery is an individual process. The problem feels personal and so the solution needs to match this. For some customers the meeting should be face-to-face or personalised in some way. Perhaps the response can recognise the number of years that the customer has been buying from the firm. A call by a director after the problem has been solved could provide another element of personal recognition. A customer who has emailed may expect a faster response than a customer who has posted a written letter of complaint. A letter of response should repeat some of the phrases used in the customer's letter rather than simply using stock phrases from standard letters.

5 Offer a choice of solutions

When the problem arose, the customer experienced losing control. This part of the recovery is placing the customer back in control. Having heard the situation the service provider offers two ways of putting things right, asking which one they would prefer. For example, you might offer a refund or a replacement product. Exercising a choice recognises the importance of the customer as party to the recovery.

6 Demonstrate fairness

Unfairness creates strong emotions and long memories. Seiders and Berry (1998) warn that because customers generally expect fair treatment, their reactions to unfairness are pronounced. Customers who are vulnerable in some way are particularly likely to be affected by unfairness perceptions. Social psychologists have shown that when people detect injustice they are motivated to restore justice. Retaliation is a common response and victims of injustice will punish the source, even at some cost to themselves. Hence it is important that the customer perceives the recovery outcome as just and fair.

> it is important that the customer perceives the recovery outcome as just and fair

Tax and Brown (1998) researched the aspect of fairness and identified three elements of fairness in service recovery:

- **Outcome fairness** – the results achieved from the complaint.
- **Process fairness** – the policies, rules and timeliness of the procedures.
- **Inter-actional fairness** – the inter-personal treatment during the process.

To achieve a fair outcome, customers expect an apology, rectification in the form of a repair or replacement, and some recognition or compensation for the inconvenience suffered. The researchers found that recovery processes are rated as fair when they are clear to the customer and the solution is quick, convenient and flexible. The interactions are perceived as fair when the behaviour of company representatives is polite, concerned and honest.

7 Keep the new promise

The service failure is a broken promise. The recovery process aims to put matters right. The organisation is making a new promise to the customer. If this falls short there is a double deviation. Therefore close attention must be paid to ensure that the new promise is kept and that the customer recognises this. Firms should follow up and monitor the rectification itself and, if need be, subsequent transactions. One bank instituted a 30-day call to customers experiencing a significant problem. Thirty days after the original problem had been fixed, a senior manager would call the customer to confirm that the matter had been resolved and that no further issues had arisen in the meantime elsewhere across the bank's services. This process reassures customers and helps them to draw a line under the problem, freeing them to place it in the past rather than seeing it as a current issue.

8 Learn from the event

Finally, the recovery from a service failure is a learning opportunity. Make sure that changes follow to prevent recurrence. The Board of Unilever receives a monthly report on emerging issues from customers, new problems and concerns of customers voiced for the first time. Customer complaints form part of the firm's scanning for ideas and improvements. In addition, it is a chance to learn and improve customer service techniques.

A world-class recovery depends on excellence at each stage. Some brands believe that brilliant service recovery is part of their success. BMW in the USA, for example, tie dealer rewards to their rating on handling dissatisfied customers.

Recovering when it isn't your fault

The problem may be created by a wholly external factor. Travel companies were not to blame for the eruption of the Eyjafjallajökull volcano in 2010. Yet because of the ash cloud European planes were grounded and holidaymakers found their travel plans disrupted. For example, Thomson Holidays were unable to fly 1400 cruise passengers from Madeira back to the United Kingdom. Instead, Thomson sailed them to Falmouth on the cruise ship *Island Escape*. Typically customer reviews on travel websites are negative and range between one and two stars (out of five). With an effective recovery strategy, Thomson achieved a series of five-star reviews for their handling of the aftermath of the volcano ash flight ban. For example, passengers on the cruise ship *Celebration* wrote:

*We cannot speak highly enough of the captain and crew of
the* Celebration, *they were absolutely brilliant and Thomson's
head office appeared to make decisions quickly and
decisively. At no point did we feel left to fend for ourselves.
Since returning home we have heard some real horror
stories about people being left to find and pay for alternative
accommodation whilst they waited on flights. We will certainly
travel with Thomsons again. It is easy to complain about
holiday operators, but the measure of a company is how they
handle difficult problems. Thomsons were first class.*

www.reviewcentre.com, 27 April 2010

Finally, helping a customer (or potential customer) when the
problem is of their own making can gain even greater kudos.
Cuba strictly enforces the requirement for Tourist entry visas.
A family were checking in at Heathrow for their flights to Cuba
but were refused boarding as they didn't have Tourist Cards.
The person behind them in the queue was a client of tailor-made
travel company Trailfinders. He mentioned that Trailfinders had
issued him with a Cuban Tourist Card in their Kensington Travel
Centre and gave them the phone number. Result: a panic phone
call followed by one of the Trailfinders visa team jumping on
his motorbike and reaching Heathrow with a handful of Cuban
Tourist Cards just in time for the family to board their plane.
Rescuing the situation resulted in a very grateful family. The drama
of the rescue story wins new customers and secures wide-scale
recommendation. People remember a good recovery.

Conclusions

Let me quote service guru Len Berry's three rules of service
recovery (Bell *et al.*, 2007, p. 130):

1. Do it right first time.
2. Fix it if it fails.
3. Remember there are no third chances.

Service recovery may restore the status quo if it is executed well. If
it is executed brilliantly, it may even achieve the service paradox
of a better outcome than before the problem arose. Either way, the

recovery is an opportunity to manage the customer perceptions upwards. Above all, perception is in the mind of the customer – if they perceive a problem then you have something to fix.

Crisis management

When a critical failure occurs, the eyes of the world are on you. Here is how US Airways responded when the spotlight was on them.

On 15 January 2009, US Airways flight 1549 from New York La Guardia to Charlotte en route for Seattle Tacoma crash-landed on the Hudson River when both engines failed, after it flew through a flock of Canada geese. All 150 passengers and all five crew survived. Captain Chesley 'Sully' Sullenberger became a hero.

Thanks to the skill and ability of the captain, US Airways had 150 wet passengers who had lost their luggage, wallets, spectacles, keys and so on. Water-soaked mobile phones do not operate and relatives were frantic with worry. How did US Airways recover this situation? Here are some of the actions they took to put matters right in the aftermath of the forced landing:

▌ Customer service immediately activated an 800 number for worried relatives to call for information

▌ The airline dispatched a care team of 100 from Headquarters at a moment's notice

▌ The Corporate Finance managing director, Scott Stewart, took a bag of emergency cash for passengers plus credit cards for employees to buy medicine, toiletries or personal items for passengers

▌ They arranged prepaid cell phones for passengers who had lost their phones in the Hudson River

▌ Dry clothes such as tracksuits were made available

▌ Warm meals were provided

▌ A task force worked on replacing lost possessions

▌ Passengers were offered new flights or hotel rooms with a round-the-clock buffet

▌ For people who did not wish to fly, train tickets or rental cars were booked. Of course, many passengers had lost their driver's licences, so a senior executive of US Airways called Hertz bosses to make sure they would allow these passengers to rent the cars without licenses.

▌ To help people return to their cars and homes, they retained locksmiths to help where keys had been lost

Once the immediate needs were covered, US Airways continued to keep in touch with passengers. A series of letters were sent refunding the air ticket cost, providing passengers with a no-quibble $5000 to replace possessions lost, plus a claim process for those whose losses exceeded this amount. In addition, every passenger received a personal letter from chairman and CEO, Doug Parker, offering them the highest frequent flier level, *Chairman's Preferred status* for 12 months. This gives passengers and a companion first-class seats when available, choice of seating and priority check-in.

As an indication of an effective recovery, more than one third of the passengers on flight 1549 flew again with US Airways in the six weeks after the forced landing.

Compiled from various sources, including *BusinessWeek*, 19 February 2009, **www.consumerist.com** and **www.usairways.com**

HOW TO APPLY

Service recovery: I can fix that

APPLICATION: MASS SERVICE

Airlines, banks, hotels, logistics firms, retailing, train-operating companies

Prevention is better than cure Considerable resources should be dedicated to spotting potential failure situations before they occur. At best, early warning will enable prevention and at worst it will permit resources to be assembled to support the recovery.

▶

Gathering a compendium of best practice In mass service businesses, with high volumes of customers, service recovery skills are an essential part of service life. When problems arise, there are often significant numbers of customers impacted. For example, weather delays to flights or train services and fire alarm activation in hotels can involve large crowds of customers. In these situations, the service staff can be performing in front of a large audience. Consequently, it is important that best practices are captured, shared and made readily available in the event that a problem arises. The compendium should list recovery situations with proven best practice responses. It should be updated regularly on the experience of new recovery situations.

For any given situation, the compendium will guide staff in safety issues, how and where to gain information, procedures to be put in place and best forms of communication to customers.

Replacing and refunding purchases The most frequent customer problem at retailers is a purchase that is either defective or not required. The customer will expect a refund or replacement. For this reason, it is important that customers are explicitly made aware if there are any constraints on returns at the time of purchase. The majority of customers will behave ethically and honestly. Software supplier Retail Equation claim that only 1% of shoppers have fraudulent or abusive return habits. Examples include wardrobing (bringing back clothing that has been worn secretly), exchanging shoplifted goods for cash, and relabelling a cheaper item as being more expensive. Return tracking systems and intelligent stock control can detect the abusers, so that the 99% can be offered lenient and flexible return policies. If in doubt, err on the side of generosity – for the honest shoppers, the return process is a daunting procedure and they will appreciate a hassle-free and helpful approach.

Face of the bank An increasing proportion of banking transactions use ATMs, automated phone services or Internet banking. Hence personal contact between staff and customers is becoming focused on new and complex transactions and complaint resolution. Thus a customer's opinion of a bank can be influenced strongly by the manner of complaint resolution. Resolution needs to be satisfactory as far as the outcome is concerned and also sensitive in terms of the process, with care being taken that there is a presumption of honesty, especially for long-term account holders.

Expert role-play Teams who have experienced particular recovery situations should role play their actions with other teams in order to share knowledge and experience. Lessons from a fellow employee who has been through a difficult recovery are very credible to other staff.

Recognition Members of staff who have successfully handled challenging recovery situations deserve recognition and praise. They need to be seen as exemplars of customer service. Sometimes the mavericks of the daily routine shine in a crisis.

APPLICATION: SERVICE SHOP

Hospitals, car repairers and travel agents

Unique needs, emotional response In these services, the interactions are more individual and customised. Each customer expects the service to be focused on their unique needs. When something goes wrong, issues relating to health, mobility and holidays generate strong emotions. In the medical arena, patients and carers experience a range of fears and concerns about illness, operations, treatments and outcomes. Worried patients and carers can behave in ways that are challenging to medical staff. Owners also become emotional when they face unexpected problems with their cars. Disappointed travellers can also overreact and become emotional. Memories of problems and their resolution are very long for all these categories, so it is important to rehearse and refine recovery procedures.

Fairness Customers and patients will often feel vulnerable because they are aware that they may not understand the medical or technical processes that lie behind a good outcome. They are in the hands of an expert, yet despite their own lack of knowledge, they expect to be treated with respect and dignity.

Managing perceptions of fairness is important. There are aspects of fair play that may be affronted. For example, in travel disruption, priority may be given to passengers with small children or to the most frequent fliers. Consideration needs to be given to ensure that any patients or customers who fall outside the priority group understand the reasons for this to avoid perceptions of unfairness.

Calming techniques Given the anger, fear and upset that can result from problems in these types of service, there is a strong requirement for skills in diffusing anger and providing reassurance. Firms/hospitals should share best practices in dealing with difficult customers/patients.

Service recovery protocols Although recovery situations can vary widely, there will be certain protocols regarding gathering of information, reporting back to customers/patients, phrasing of bad news and so on. These should be recorded, updated, easily available for reference and used in training.

APPLICATION: PROFESSIONAL SERVICE

Accountants, architects, consultants, doctors and lawyers

Every client situation will be unique and so the resolution to any problem will be individual and customised. Solutions should be based on recovering from the failure and rebuilding trust.

Billing errors Prevention is better than cure, but when a billing error occurs it is extremely important to double-check future invoices for a period of say six months to ensure that a second billing error does not compound the first one.

Involvement of senior partners When a problem has occurred, restoration of trust is paramount. A good practice is to have a senior person to make a 30-day courtesy call, to ensure that all is well on a continuing basis after resolution. It may be appropriate for the senior person to maintain 'light-touch' contact for some months as a means to rebuild long-term confidence.

Staying ahead – service innovation

Pick the odd word out from the following list:

   systematic, consistent, routine, exciting, reliable, dependable

Yes, the odd one out is 'exciting'. The essence of good service is consistent reliability and great service providers successfully target customer perceptions every time. However, there is a drawback – routine is not exciting, systematic is not interesting. In time customers may fail to notice good service, taking it for granted. Familiarity becomes lack of interest, which can descend into boredom. The customer becomes vulnerable to a new provider – not through any lack of effective performance, but simply through indifference.

Over time, competitors can monitor your service, recruit your trained staff, match your specifications and replicate the key elements. Differences become marginal. Or competitors may choose in times of recession to cut their prices. Your 'slightly better' offering begins to look expensive. This leads to a sense of market commoditisation where the only advantages are lower price or greater convenience. The answer is service innovation, as shown in Figure A7.1.

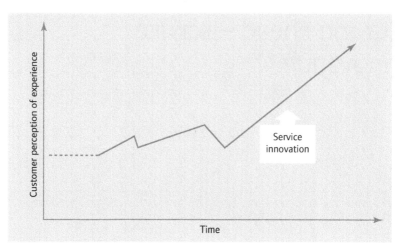

FIGURE A7.1 Satisfaction curve – service innovation

Service redesign

Create and offer an entirely new service or undertake a redesign of the existing service. Leonard Berry and Sandra Lampo (2000) set out a framework for service redesign, with five possible approaches, described below.

1 Self-service

This moves the customer from receiver to part producer. This can increase customer perceptions of control, allowing the user to choose the timing and the speed of service delivery. Waiting time may be reduced. Service firms introducing high technology, for example to support Internet self-service, can enhance their reputation for modernity as well as reducing transaction costs.

> training and incentives may be required to make customers aware, willing and competent to serve themselves

However, there are drawbacks in extending self-service. For example, training and incentives may be required to make customers aware, willing and competent to serve themselves. This has been the case with supermarket self-scanning systems. Another drawback is the reduction in direct customer contact. Checking-in for a flight online is faster, cheaper and more convenient, yet customers miss out on the advice and interaction with the check-in staff and airlines lose the informal feedback.

2 Direct service

This brings the service to the customer rather than requiring the customer to come to the service location. Direct service can expand the customer base because the company is going beyond its existing locations. Customer convenience is improved and customers who place a high value on time will appreciate the benefit.

The provider may face system investment and additional operating costs for delivering this added convenience.

3 Pre-service

This streamlines the initiation process through some form of registration, form-completion, prepayment or communication of special requests, so that the customer can speed through the service process. Pre-service increases the ability to personalise services, improves speed for the customer and enhances efficiency for the service provider.

The only drawbacks are those associated with many innovations – making customers aware of the new process and training staff to implement the new methods in parallel with the old system for non-registered customers.

4 Bundled service

This involves creating a package or bundle of services as a single offering. Different packages can be offered to different segments of customers. Present a comprehensive pack in contrast to a menu-based approach where everything is paid for as it is used. The benefits to the customer are added convenience and the opportunity to sample additional aspects of the service on an inclusive basis. This may increase satisfaction. For the firm it allows the potential to charge higher prices and increase service utilisation.

The challenge is to understand the customer well enough to define the packages and prices in such a way that they appeal to customers and deliver profitable returns.

5 Physical service

This focuses attention on the physical aspects of the service, such as the communication materials, premises, the lighting, the tickets, the employees and their uniforms. The service itself may be intangible, but the customer can judge the quality of the seats and the wallpaper. Customers may draw positive conclusions from redesigned service furniture and décor, and it may spark interest and stimulate word-of-mouth comments. For the firm, there is evidence that paying attention to the service environment enhances staff motivation and also pre-disposes customers to behave in a more considerate manner.

The drawbacks of investing in physical collateral of service is the absolute cost and the low barriers to competitor imitation.

Create interest, differentiate from rivals

Service redesign is a major undertaking. There are benefits of smaller innovations. New ideas and extra twists can create interest. A few years ago, the UK-based Automobile Association (AA), which provides services to motorists, briefed all their employees that a core objective was to 'impress customers a little more every time'. The AA recognised that staying with the norm was not enough to retain business in a competitive market. Whatever mechanics or phone agents had offered the motorist on a previous occasion, they needed to go a little further this time. Adding novelty gives the customer something to notice, something to mention to their friends. In effect firms are improving value in an appeal to logic and improving variety in an appeal to emotions (see Figure A7.2).

> adding novelty gives the customer something to notice

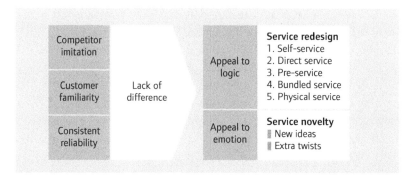

FIGURE A7.2 Need for innovation

A stream of small innovations can even contribute to winning a customer's loyalty. A feeling that the service is always getting better leads to faith in the future. Customers may even disregard competitor blandishments because they do not want to risk missing the next intriguing enhancement. Take a runner, for example, who can choose Nike, Reebok or Adidas, among other brands. The introduction of the Nike+ created excitement among runners: using their iPod and Nike+ shoes they can track their runs and monitor their improvement, using the data stored on the iPod, which plays music as they jog. Then Nike adds another feature like the ability to record on a map the route that was taken. Next appears another facility, the scope to add personal resolutions, or a training programme in preparation for a half-marathon. Each new application to this information service increases a runner's adherence to the Nike brand. The next pair of shoes will be Nike too.

In another sector, led by CEO Justin King, the supermarket Sainsbury's follows this strategy with the tag line 'Try something new today'. A stream of new products supports the strategy. Merchandising makes customers notice. The company offers recipes with an unusual twist like serving salmon with baby courgettes and pumpkin seeds. They suggest creative food combination ideas such as adding a slice of apple and cucumber to an elderflower drink, or stirring raspberries into breakfast porridge. Research by Tom Roach and Craig Mawdsley of advertising agency AMV.BBDO indicates that around 10 million customers have picked up a recipe card and 4 million customers claim to use a Sainsbury's food idea at least once a month (Dawson, 2009). Following the launch of the idea,

Sainsbury's experienced ten consecutive quarters of growth with over half of that coming from existing customers. Feedback from consumer research included encouraging comments such as: 'It's very clever because they're not just advertising Sainsbury's – they're giving you an idea' and 'Cooking can be so boring sometimes – anything that helps liven things up is definitely welcome'. Innovation that creates interest or helps customers to succeed will add another dimension.

In business-to-business, one of the world-leading suppliers to the global food industry has employed a successful strategy of regular innovation to differentiate from rivals. Alongside product innovation, this company has provided enhanced services and technical support. This has included guidance to customers on wastage minimisation and ideal product characteristics for finished food appearance, cooking capability and mouth-feel. These innovative added value services offer greater benefits to customers and enable the business to command higher prices in the market place and increase customer loyalty.

> innovative added-value services offer greater benefits to customers

Effective communication with customers reinforces the value of being a customer. According to JD Power and Associates, 82% of cardholders with American Express are aware of the benefits and services associated with their card, compared with an industry average of only 70%. American Express customers also report having access to an average of approximately five benefits and services, compared with the industry average of less than three. JD Power commented in their 2009 credit card satisfaction survey that this awareness is an important contributor to the high level of satisfaction with rewards and benefits among American Express customers, compared with other credit card issuers.

Speed to market

Some service enhancements can be implemented speedily. Product improvements normally take time to identify and require design input, testing and refinement with a schedule to change production methods. Service changes have a shorter gestation period. Service and experience enhancements, can be conceived, piloted and implemented very rapidly. When these ideas are linked to a distinctive competence, they will be much more difficult to imitate.

The best service systems operate with well-honed processes, delivered through properly trained staff. This means that intuitively, organisations prefer to introduce a number of innovations at one stroke. In this way they can phase in a new system and a revised training protocol. Yet, to create a perception of a constant stream of innovations in the mind of the user, it is more effective to bring in one change at a time, adding a follow-on innovation when customers have digested the first change. The time length between innovations in this approach will depend on the frequency of the typical customer usage pattern. Ideally a firm should possess agility and use systems that are flexible to cope with enhancements, and find quick ways to update staff on new concepts.

The service innovation process

So what is the best process for service innovation? The following list shows the six steps:

1. Scouring for insights.
2. Developing new value propositions.
3. Piloting ideas with real customers.
4. Reviewing – learning from failure, refining successes.
5. Roll-out.
6. Monitoring the results.

1 Scouring for insights

Insights are specific discoveries about customers that create opportunities to innovate ahead of competitors (see Figure A7.3). Observing the aspects that give a customer real pleasure or pride can lead to insights. According to Michael I. Norton (2009), writing

FIGURE A7.3 Scouring for insights

in *Harvard Business Review*, once customers have mastered a self-assembly skill, they become so proud of their efforts that they rate the results more highly than professionally produced items. He calls this the 'Ikea effect'. The insight is that creating a part-completed product or experience allows the customer to finalise it or tailor it to his or her own requirements. Imagine part-baked garlic bread which customers unwrap, place on a baking tray and enjoy the results 20 minutes later. Starbucks have employed the same technique in encouraging customers to make increasingly sophisticated personal choices in the coffee bean variety, number of espresso shots, type of milk and added flavours. Physical service operations have the advantage that customers can be observed during the process. It is possible to discern their degree of delight from their expressions and demeanour. They are accessible for research.

It is also easy to ask a customer of a service for feedback at the end of the encounter. Many hotels and restaurants ask guests the question 'Was everything OK?' Author Jill Griffin (2002) suggests that a more insightful angle comes from the question posed by a Renaissance Hotel in Orlando, Florida: 'What's one thing we could have done better to improve your stay?'

Negative elimination is another source of insight. In 1986 Sinclair Beecham and Julian Metcalfe conceived the UK sandwich chain, Prêt a Manger. Their inspiration came from listing all the things that annoyed customers and getting rid of them. They eliminated sell-by dates and stale bread by making up fresh sandwiches every day, distributing unsold stock to the homeless every evening. In 2006, Sinclair Beecham followed the same process in designing the Hoxton Hotel in Shoreditch, East London. He investigated the features of hotels that customers found irritating and devised a solution to obviate them. For instance, real milk is provided with tea trays instead of irksome sealed pots of UHT milk.

complainers are usually better educated than average buyers

Complaining customers are also a source of potential insight. At Disney World the garbage collectors are the group most often approached by guests with complaints and comments. Disney listens to the garbage collectors. Complainers are usually better educated than average buyers. They may be more committed to the brand and genuinely care about improving it. Therefore a retail bank recruited a user-group of people who had complained in the past, in order to consult with them about new products and services. Brokers Charles Schwab listened to comments from customers. The company had successfully moved many customers from branch to telephone service. One snag emerged: in a branch the customer with an additional question can readily return to the same representative who served him or her originally. This is not possible with phone agents – once the phone has been hung up, the customer has to start afresh with a new representative. In 2008, Schwab instituted a direct dial feature that allows customers to call back the representative they were dealing with, rather than navigating the automated menu-based phone system a second time.

Logically, heavy users are a favourable source of innovative ideas, simply because they will be rather familiar with the service operation that they patronise regularly. They may have a closer relationship with operators and therefore be willing to invest time in focus groups and to share their views openly. The opposite groups may also provide stimulating thoughts. Why are light-users only buying infrequently? What might tempt them to increase their business? Chan Kim and Renee Mauborgne (2005) in their book *Blue Ocean Strategy* cite non-users as a vital group to consult for groundbreaking ideas. Why are they *not* buying? What inhibits them? For example, which types of people avoid circuses and how could Cirque du Soleil transform their version of circus to appeal to these non-attenders?

One particular category of customers is especially valuable in identifying insights. Research by Eric von Hippel (1986) identified a group of 10–40% of customers he named 'lead users'. These are customers who identify new potential requirements months or even years before the main market and have a vested interest in finding or developing a solution to these needs. As an illustration, a small number of windsurfers engage in developing or modifying their boards. They suggest or create innovations that manufacturers can usefully adopt and integrate into new products. They are ahead of the adoption curve because they are in effect pre-adopters. Top athletes are the lead users who help Nike to evolve new concepts of sports shoes. Service lead users often identify themselves by emailing or writing suggestions for service improvements. Relationships with these lead users are valuable because they offer advance warning of emerging needs. Service firms can work with lead users to develop and test solutions to garner competitive advantage.

Insights from employees

Front-line servers see customers in context. Capture their impressions and ideas. Make it easy for them to offer suggestions and contribute improvements. Some senior executives build time into their diaries to work alongside front-liners so that they can engage with customers directly and discuss the outcomes with the front-liners. Malaysian entrepreneur Tony Fernandes, who founded Air Asia, spends one day every two months as cabin crew on one of Air Asia's 80 planes. Every three months he spends a day working on check-in. The insight he gains from customers and crews has helped him build an award-winning airline. Unusually for an Asian business, the firm's lack of hierarchy means that new ideas reach decision-makers quickly.

New employees will have first impressions. Interview them six weeks after joining the business. Before they become fully normalised through the induction process, give them the opportunity to share their ideas, thoughts and observations. Some questions are shown in Figure A7.4.

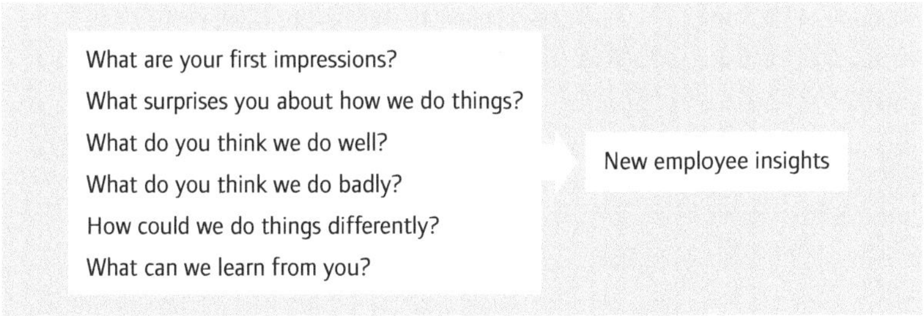

> What are your first impressions?
>
> What surprises you about how we do things?
>
> What do you think we do well?
>
> What do you think we do badly?
>
> How could we do things differently?
>
> What can we learn from you?

New employee insights

FIGURE A7.4 Insights from new employees

Some comments may be irrelevant, unaffordable or off-beam. This doesn't matter, because among the impractical and mundane could be some transforming gems.

Learn from your suppliers

Your suppliers have a vested interest in your success. Some will be set in their ways and others more creative. Evaluate your suppliers on a 1–10 scale of inventiveness and liveliness and talk to those who score 8 and above. Share with them some of the challenges posed by demanding customers. Invite them to discuss industry changes with you and propose potential developments. Create a joint improvement team of your bright high-fliers and their rising stars, challenging them to come up with solutions for specific opportunities. The process will improve relationships. The supplier also benefits by learning more about your business, specifically gaining a line-of-sight to his customer's customer.

Concepts from other countries

Travel broadens the mind; so inquire what is happening in your service sector in markets far from your own. How does a Brazilian car recovery man placate a motorist who has waited an hour for rescue? Answer: by presenting a cake 'to eat while I fix your car'. How does an Australian filling station avoid angering customers who fill their cars with petrol just before a price drop? Answer: in Western Australia they notify their 'tomorrow price' by 2 p.m. each day. How does a Japanese hospital improve patient experience? Answer: by involving an office furniture manufacturer to design solutions to difficulties faced by patients such as finding their way around the hospital and frustrations with waiting. The solution even incorporated modular elements updated seasonally for added appeal to returning patients.

Look to the most demanding markets in the world for your ideas. For an architect wanting to learn about lighting, go to the Royal Institute of Technology (KTH) in Stockholm. The Architectural Lighting Design Program has to be excellent because Swedish people claim to be more conscious of light than any other nation.

Learn from other service industries

How do other industries do it? Make exchange visits to other businesses to share ideas on how to serve customers. Executives from Friesland Foods, the Dutch cheese-maker, visited leading Dutch businesses – from retailing and brewing to insurance and car-washing – seeking applicable innovative ideas in an initiative called 'Steal with Pride'. Lexus in the USA regularly invites their dealers to business summits with other companies such as Apple. Following the summit with Apple some dealers began offering special help desks for high-tech automotive gadgets. If you are in business-to-business then look at consumer markets and vice versa. Keep minds open to translating ideas from another sector into your market.

2 Developing new value propositions

The insight leads to new answers. Good creative advice says that you should not stop thinking with your first answer, rather to seek further and better answers that lead to an original solution. Challenging the concept is important. The proposal to install ironing equipment in every Marriott bedroom was based on analysis of the number of requests for irons and the cost of associate time in delivering irons to bedrooms. The outcome from an insight is an enhanced value proposition.

The value proposition combines together the benefits to the customer in terms of advantage, convenience, risk reduction, reassurance and emotional payback with the cost in money, time and effort to the customer. It summarises the tangibles and intangibles of the deal. For example, a restaurant offering a free child's meal with every adult meal is providing both benefits – the tangible cash saving of a free child meal and the emotional reassurance that children are welcome here.

Enhancing the value proposition means giving customers or clients an added reason to try your product or service. What is the incremental benefit? Examples are greater timesaving, easier access, improved compatibility with other systems, raised customer status, higher priority, or a contribution to a better environment. Can you help the customer to feel better physically, to feel more confident or more empowered?

> enhancing the value proposition means giving customers or clients an added reason to try your product or service

Service value propositions are often hard to visualise where the added benefit is as intangible as an emotional feeling. Tangible elements can be incorporated into a mock-up or a prototype model. However, the development team may need to role play the improved experience or script a scenario. For example, when many patients seek appointments to see their general practitioners (local doctors), there will be a delay for an appointment. An improved value proposition could be to offer phone appointments in certain circumstances (perhaps to provide a test result). The phone appointment can save time for both patient and doctor and be equally effective. To envisage how this would work, the surgery might develop a phone role play for a typical test feedback, to show the way reassurance and answers can be provided over the phone. An internal test with employees or staff is known as an alpha test and would include safety testing.

Improved value to customers may derive from lowering costs as well as increasing benefits. In recessionary times, the value proposition may need to be enhanced by greater efficiency. For example, Marriott Hotels are cross-training administrators so that they have the skills to serve at banquets – this maintains high service levels without having to hire more staff. The International Customer Management Institute (ICMI) warns service providers about eliminating customer service agents. An ICMI study in 2008 showed that eliminating four representatives in a call centre of 36 agents might increase the number of customers put on hold for four minutes from zero to 80 (McGregor, 2009, p 28). The United Services Automobile Association (USAA), the financial services company serving the United States military, considered this. Rather than eliminating people, USAA cross-trained their people to be able to cover multiple tasks. This saved time with fewer transfers between agents and improved productivity.

3 Piloting with real customers

Value exists in the mind of the customer. Therefore the enhanced value proposition must be tested in a trial with real customers. Assumptions and views of customer-facing staff are a guide but checking the validity with a paying customer is a vital step. The initial trial with a customer is known as a beta test.

Some retailers have pilot stores and restaurant chains have test-bed locations to try new concepts. If there is an element of uncertainty about the effectiveness of the new method, the customer should obviously be warned and participate voluntarily. Business-to-business firms know their clients and can identify willing guinea pigs for a test version of a new approach. Some companies run joint trials with their customers. For example, Cargill Industrial Starches have a pilot coating plant at their Application and Development Centre in Krefeld, Germany where they test new forms of coatings for paper. In fact this facility is now offered as a testing service to customers seeking improved flexibility and runnability without costs of complexity.

The test may be focused precisely on one segment of customers. For example, LloydsTSB Bank tested and then installed hearing induction loop systems in all branches to enhance their service to hearing impaired customers. Additional actions included deaf-awareness training for customer-facing staff, subtitles on television advertisements through teletext and textphone numbers being listed in letters and leaflets. This approach resulted in the award of a 'Louder than Words' Chartermark from the Royal National Institute for the Deaf.

4 Reviewing – learning from failure, refining success

Some service experiments will fail. The benefit of a rapid pilot with real customers is quick learning. Fast failure uses very little resource and moves the firm towards more successful directions. For example, Google noted the popularity of the virtual world 'Second Life' and developed its own version of a virtual environment called 'Lively'. It was launched in July 2008. When fast learning indicated that it was failing, Google closed it down only four months later. The firm was able to place new resources into ventures with better potential. Fast failure is a key part of innovation.

Some new service tests will succeed immediately. Most will fall in-between and require some form of refinement or redevelopment before they are rolled out. There may be technical adjustments to make. Operationally, an innovation will need misuse and abuse testing to be effective when used by inexpert or careless customers. Normal customers in routine usage have found no problems, but before the innovation is extended it is important to evaluate the extremes of usage. In this instance, employees will be invited to 'destruction test' a new piece of kit or modified system. How will the process respond to ten times the forecast load?

It is wise to use customer experience to refine instructions, warnings and signals. Which symbols worked well and which were misunderstood? Where did customers appear frustrated and where did they smile? How could we speed up the process of understanding for customers?

What questions did customers ask? What answers satisfied them most effectively?

Companies often seem to speak a different language from customers. It is more formal and uses technical jargon. For example, banks provide the facility of an automated teller machine (ATM), but customers get money from cashpoints. Therefore listen carefully to the words and phrases customers use to explain or advise another customer. How do customers describe the enhanced service to potential buyers? What forms of communication convey the new benefits most clearly?

Finally, pricing is a factor to consider before roll-out. How highly was the innovation valued? There may be an opportunity to price up where the test customers were delighted. Conversely, it may be necessary to review communication messages or the new pricing level if the value of the enhancement is seen as marginal.

5 Roll-out

The roll-out must be planned to be effective. Confirm the value proposition and brief the change clearly to employees. What is the new deal? What are the winning benefits? Which segments or types of customer will appreciate the new approach? How should they handle change? A good briefing includes the questions that were raised by customers and the model answers.

Launching a new offer feels risky. Make heroes of early adopters among employees. Who are the most influential store managers, client directors and customer relationship managers? Encourage the opinion leaders in your organisation to back the new way of doing business.

Customer communications need to be handled with care. Service innovations are hard to communicate, especially if the change is intangible. Sometimes the changes may seem more significant to employees than they appear to customers. Or the benefits feel better to customers in practice than they would imagine from hearing about them from an advertisement beforehand. Whilst it is important not to undersell your innovation, advertising can appear to over-promise. Often the advertising is most effective when it generates traffic and sampling on a wider scale. Seek the experimental customers and the innovators. Better to gain and publicise positive feedback and encourage word-of-mouth recommendation. This is likely to have a greater impact in selling the new proposition.

6 Monitoring the results

Service operations thrive on precise and demanding measures of effectiveness.

Routine processes lend themselves to ratios and comparisons. Examples are average call length, stock-turn ratios, number of covers and revenue per employee.

Be warned that introducing new propositions depresses some of the standard ratios initially. For instance, it may take longer to sell in a package. It may be expensive running the new system in parallel with the old. Allow training time. Customer throughput will slow before it speeds up, when time is invested in pre-service data capture. Take care not to punish the employees who are succeeding with the innovation. Set and celebrate targets for adoption of the new value proposition.

Use the metrics to go further. Let the results stimulate the hunt for new insights, leading to the next service innovation.

The adoption of service innovations

Innovation diffusion can be slower than expected. A small number of experimental customers will welcome the novelty. An example is the wave of early adopters into electronic banking. This can be misleading, because the majority of customers are risk-averse, exhibiting caution about the unfamiliar. For these customers the novelty element is actually discouraging. Evidence exists that they prefer a positioning that highlights the continuity and reduces the perceived risk of trial. They are influenced by tangibles that give confidence. They take note of recommendations from satisfied users.

Service innovation is essential to stay ahead of competitors. For the early adopter customers, it is appropriate to highlight the specific novelty to motivate and enthuse them. For the majority of customers, it is the actual experience of a rising curve of service delivery that delights them.

> service innovation is essential to stay ahead of competitors

Service innovation in professional service

Clients commission professional service companies to give them information and advice. In Spain, an oil company commissioned market research to help executives understand shopper behaviour and to inform their marketing decisions. The company they chose was Kantar Worldpanel, whose continuous syndicated consumer panels make it the world's leading provider of research into shoppers' purchase and usage behaviour.

In 2008, the oil company ran a promotion with a leading food retailer, where for every €10 of grocery shopping, customers received a fuel discount voucher worth 6 cents/litre at filling stations, up to a maximum of 20 litres. The oil company asked Kantar Worldpanel to interrogate the data from their panel of fuel buyers and evaluate the promotion. There was good news – the promotion had increased custom.

Then came the service innovation! Kantar Worldpanel analysed data supplied by their petrol buyers and fast-moving consumer goods panels, and uncovered two strategic insights:

▌ Insight 1: drivers typically buy 25 to 60 litres of fuel per visit, so the limit of 20 litres acts as an inhibitor. The typical hypermarket discount of 10 cents per litre was another inhibitor.

▌ Insight 2: The oil company's fuel customers typically spend more on fresh products than the average grocery shopper.

For 2009, Kantar Worldpanel proposed a creative two-way concept designed to increase the loyalty of customers and to raise their spend at both grocery store *and* filling station. Presented as 12 cents per litre, it rewarded grocery customers with fuel vouchers for every €15 spent, and rewarded fuel customers with grocery vouchers for every 20 litres of fuel bought.

Kantar Worldpanel presented this new strategy to both parties with data and analysis. The promotion was agreed and implemented. The business results – in tougher market conditions – were impressive for both companies.

In professional service, good service helps your client to make money. But to help your client make money for another organisation as well is real service innovation.

HOW TO APPLY

Service innovation: I can fix that

Airlines, banks, hotels, logistics firms, retailing, train-operating companies

Service innovation context For service operations covering a mass of customers, such as retail, rail travel, flights and hotel services, the scale of infrastructure and physical equipment is daunting. Shell operates 56,000 filling stations in 90 countries. Indian Railways has 6900 stations. JP Morgan Chase has over 5000 bank branches, Intercontinental operates 3300 hotel properties and the Lufthansa fleet has more than 500 planes. To introduce an enhancement to physical aspects requires a large budget, a systematic plan and the roll-out takes time. Similarly, to make a difference to the intangible experience through staff behaviour towards customers, needs training investment and time to implement. Effective change management processes are vital to achieve results from initiatives. Any change must be tested thoroughly before roll-out.

Mass service businesses have an insight goldmine through being able to observe many customers in the service process. Seeing your customers and the way they buy – or do not buy – creates an immense opportunity. For example, Zara, the international clothing retailer, provides their store staff around the world with hand-held communication devices to send feedback on trends to HQ and the designers from customer interaction. What are customers seeking, what do they reject? Retailers such as B&Q identify emerging segments such as 'do-it-for-me' rather than 'do-it-yourself'. Installation services for the segment that want the work done for them can then be developed.

Customers judge first on fundamental criteria such as availability, on-time service and cleanliness. If the basics are satisfactory, customers frequently take services for granted. Innovation therefore provides a way of creating positive notice of the service. Small enhancements make people feel the service is improving and gives them something positive to talk about after the journey/stay.

Direction for innovation The most effective approach to innovation in these types of business is volume idea generation and assessment. Instil processes to generate a large number of ideas for potential enhancements using customer complaints, feedback and suggestions, employee suggestion schemes and external trawling for ideas. Idea generation sessions can focus on the different stages of the journey in turn, beginning with improvement to the pre-journey experience and ending with the aftermath. Ideas generated must be screened against ten criteria:

1. Value and importance of perceived benefit from customer viewpoint.

2. Ease of communication to customers.

3. Potential to stimulate positive word-of-mouth comments.

4. The potential angles for media comment.

5. Financial cost of introduction.

6. Management effort required for successful introduction.

7. Timescale for roll-out.

8. Risks of introduction.

9. Potential customer disappointment if it has to be discontinued.

10. Ability to differentiate from any competitor copying the idea.

These criteria will identify effective ideas for constant improvement of the offer or the customer experience. Many will be minor and some may represent occasional positive surprises for customers who see them as a one-off benefit. An airline might celebrate 16 April and 19 August as the birthdays of Wilbur and Orville Wright, the pioneer aviators. A rail company could collaborate with a food manufacturer launching a new product and offer a sample as a complimentary snack.

A hotel company could institute a systematic approach to encourage staff to thank staff on departure. The aim is low cost and high impact.

Retail innovation is vital, yet retail relationships with suppliers are often characterised as adversarial, where retailers place heavy pressure on suppliers to cut prices, particularly in tougher trading situations. This can be a short-term approach since it starves innovation of investment. Suppliers with innovative products find it beneficial to offer them first to the retailers who have a more collaborative approach. Developing new processes across the supply chain requires trust and a willingness to experiment together. Thus the more aggressive approach with suppliers has counterbalancing consequences with customers.

Customer benefit is the important consideration. How can you offer improving value to customers? One way is to help customers make sense of the future and reduce uncertainty for them. Carphone Warehouse identified that customers were holding back from buying new phones because they were concerned lest the price may come down after the purchase had been made. The innovation from this insight was to create the Ultimate Price Promise. If the price for the handset on the same network and tariff is higher than the price listed in the following month's *Buyers Guide*, then Carphone Warehouse will send a credit voucher for the difference. The customer is protected from a price drop, but in return the retailer gains permission to communicate additional offers to the customer by direct marketing. It is a win for the retailer and a win for the customer.

Another trend for consumers in mass service is 'help-me-choose'. In situations where the customer is overwhelmed by a plethora of choices, advice and guidance is necessary in order to come out with the right answer. The trend is to develop a series of analytical questions (in person or via the Internet) that progressively narrow the choice options for the customer, to eliminate unsuitable products and finally identify the product that suits the customer's needs.

Segmentation by value Where new ideas are expensive to introduce and appear to have a high payback, the most effective approach is to launch them initially to the current and potential high-value customers. For example, Airlines and hotels have frequent flier clubs and rail companies have databases of season ticket holders. This special attention is a positive reward for the most loyal customers. Depending on the results, the ideas can be rolled out to the remaining customers.

Cost efficiency Identify savings that do not impact on customer experience. For example, Ritz-Carlton hotels retimed laundry operations to run at night using lower-cost electricity. The hotel company also replaced vases of expensive cut flowers with longer-lasting exotic pot plants.

Innovation can be deployed to save costs and still meet customer needs. BMW in the USA has rolled out wi-fi to all their franchised dealers. This offers customers a cheap way of passing the time while their car is serviced. As a result, customers can use waiting time more productively. The reduced cost of operating loan cars has cut expenses by 10–15%.

APPLICATION: SERVICE SHOP

Hospitals, car repairers and travel agents

Service innovation context These service businesses have customers and patients who differ considerably and expect appropriate treatment for themselves. There are often high degrees of emotion involved in holidays, car repair and hospitalisation. Memories are laid down deeply when emotions are involved and this gives challenges to service providers.

Direction for innovation The service innovation process is tailored to this type of business

1 Categorise major types of customer/patient and determine the collective expectations of each group. For example, Accident and Emergency patients differ in their expectations from pregnant mothers and again from those diagnosed with heart disease. Customers with car warranty claims are very different from drivers needing body repairs for their vehicle.

2 Determine the stages of the experience. What is the very first part of the experience? What steps do customers go through? What is the very final stage? Map the journey through the service for the typical patient/customer.

3 Analyse and survey the customer/patient experience for each group. It can be helpful to follow customers/patients through the stages or to ask them to keep a diary of what happened and how they felt.

4 Develop enhancements for critical stages in the process. The aim is to reduce worry and concern at each point. Identify areas where changes yield a significant payback. Help customers and patients emerge from the experience feeling that they have been treated fairly and with respect and that their outcome is the best available.

These approaches will generate positive improvements to the service journey. Ideas generated include placing visible seats in long hospital corridors so that old or infirm people can rest on the way to their appointment. Provide arms to the chairs so that they can push themselves up again. Site hooks or racks at the end of the seats, so that walking sticks are retained and do not fall over as a trip hazard to others. Anything to make a hospital seem more homely and less like an institution pleases long-stay patients. Likewise, travel agents can identify different types of traveller for different experiences. For example, travellers booking to attend sports events will appreciate specific follow-up about tickets for future events. Customers who repeatedly book the same hotel each year need less pre-holiday information than first-timers to the resort.

Accountants, architects, consultants, doctors, lawyers

Service innovation context A reputation for thought leadership and professional initiatives contributes to the success of professional services business. New ideas and approaches successfully applied are valuable in differentiating from rival firms. Since 2006, the *Financial*

APPLICATION: PROFESSIONAL SERVICE

Times has organised an annual Innovative Lawyers Report with specific awards. The Report scrutinises legal expertise. For example, in 2009 one research question focused on legal innovation to mitigate the effects of recession in commercial life, another looked at new approaches to handling or helping to detect, prevent or manage fraud for clients. However, the Report goes beyond legal innovation to look for new methods in resourcing, changed practices in billing and fees, and delivering value to clients through service. Innovation is a part of achieving thought leadership

Direction for innovation Innovation in professional services goes beyond new products and embraces revising processes, introducing automation, experimenting with communication, seeking new billing systems, leveraging databases, changing the way you do business.

Risk and reward Professional services firms are well aware of the risks of change and the damage to their reputation of an initiative that fails. However, the risks of not doing something are less often calibrated. Consider the consequences of being second to a rival in two or three initiatives. The consequence is to be labelled the follower. Top clients prefer to work with leaders rather than followers.

Leaving your customers wanting more – the finishing touch

Respice finem

There is a short poem by the seventeenth-century English poet, Francis Quarles, called *Respice finem*. The Latin title means look to the end, consider the ending, think of the outcome. Its final line concludes, 'The last act crowns the play'. In service it is the ending that counts. It is the final opportunity to influence the customer perception. And as the last part of the encounter, it should be the finishing touch that leaves the customer positive, willing to speak favourably and wanting to repeat the experience (see Figure A8.1).

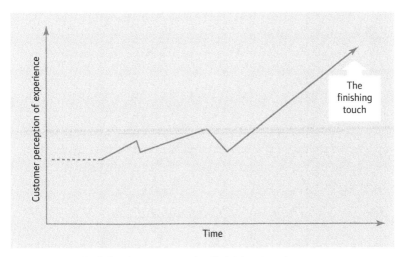

FIGURE A8.1 Satisfaction curve – the finishing touch

Kano model

Service research in the 1980s by Professor Noriaki Kano of the University of Tokyo established that the technical outcome of a service and the level of customer satisfaction needed to be separated in service analysis (Kano *et al.*, 1984). Customers could have their needs met and still be unsatisfied. He developed an analytical tool for customer satisfaction, known as the Kano model. This has two axes: the *x* axis has a scale of how well the service fulfils the customer needs in terms of outcomes, and the *y* axis indicates progress from dissatisfaction through neutral to satisfaction (see Figure A8.2). He identified six attributes that have a bearing on service satisfaction. Three of these are substantive:

▋ **Basic attributes** Must-have prerequisites for the service. These factors will not in themselves satisfy if they are fulfilled or even exceeded, but their absence will dissatisfy. For example, in a dentist's waiting room, the customer expects chairs, would be disappointed to wait standing up, but expensive leather loungers will not add to the satisfaction.

▋ **Performance attributes** Features which the customer expects and where greater performance results in higher satisfaction. The performance factor can cause pleasure or disappointment at each extreme. For example, the reassuring manner of the dentist creates patient confidence – the more reassured the patient, the greater the satisfaction.

▋ **Delighter attributes** Factors for excitement where presence causes unexpected delight and absence does not cause disappointment because they were not foreseen. For example, being presented after the treatment with a toothbrush precisely proportioned for your mouth to make teeth cleaning easier and more effective.

In addition he found three less substantive attributes:

▋ **Indifferent attributes** Factors where the customer does not value the feature. If a dentist were to provide recommendations of local tradesmen, this is unlikely to be valued by most customers.

■ **Questionable attributes** Factors where it is unclear whether it is expected by the customer and results are contradictory. Showing live sports results in a dentist's waiting room may be welcomed by some customers and unwelcome to others.

■ **Reverse attributes** Where the customer expected the opposite. Silly jokes from the surgeon? Patients may prefer a more serious approach.

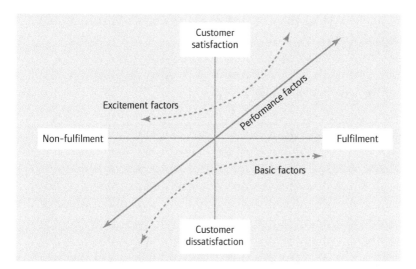

FIGURE A8.2 Kano model of customer satisfaction

Source: Kano *et al*., 1984. Reproduced by permission of Dr. N. Kano, Kano Quality Research Institute

There are four conclusions from this thinking:

1 **Refresh customer understanding constantly** Great service providers need a clear and up-to-date understanding, by segment, of the specific attributes that are currently valued by customers, and those that would be valued by customers. Know what the customer expects.

2 **Hit the basic standards** Great service providers need to understand the basic pre-requisites and to deliver them to the level of expectation. Furthermore they need to guard against over-delivery that adds to costs without being appreciated by customers.

3 **Excel at the performance factors** Identify factors that correlate directly with customer satisfaction and invest in them, to deliver higher performance, faster delivery and greater value to the customer. Be aware that competitors will also be trying to improve the same factors. It is hard to gain a service edge here, but equally it is important not to be left behind.

4 **Find positive surprises – especially at the end of the encounter** Look for unexpected aspects of the service that delight customers. These often come into play when the customer has seen that the basic attributes are in place and the expected performance is on track. As the service comes to a close the customer is moving to a positive frame of mind and an unexpected bonus can delight.

Behavioural science

The latest thinking in customer service now focuses on behavioural science. This tells us that customers remember an experience not in the manner of a moment-by-moment video recording, but rather as a series of 'memory snapshots' of highs and lows. The overall perception is determined by the quality and sequence of these snapshots. For best results, you need a higher quantity of positive snapshots and/or high impact snapshots and/or memorable snapshots as the encounter comes to a close. The factor of recency means that, perceptually, the ending is crucial. A strong finish is vital in a service encounter.

How not to do it

Many airlines give a strong start to the experience with well-trained smiling staff welcoming you to baggage drop or explaining cheerfully how the self-serve check-in works. There is a warm greeting by the aircrew as you board. But picture the end of a passenger flight:

You are ordered to sit upright, fold away your tray table, switch off iPods and fasten your safety belt. After landing there is a staccato message of welcome to your arrival city. Passengers are eager to stand up before the seat belt light flashes off. They perform unlikely contortions half-standing under overhead luggage racks, with an armrest digging into a buttock. As passengers file out, the cabin crew say a robotic farewell to 250 passengers. You queue through immigration and then find yourself alone in the baggage hall with no idea where or when your bags will appear. Will you find them? And as you worry, the happy smiling crew walks past you, joking to themselves!

How delighted will you feel with this experience?

It could be so different

Here is another way:

As the plane taxis to the gate, the crew ask all passengers to stay seated to hear a short and up-to-date briefing about the arrival and any special procedures to expect. On screen is a view of the terminal and the baggage hall. The briefing continues with information about currency exchange and onward travel and even weather conditions. The briefing ends and there is a countdown to the doors opening. The cabin crew say 'see you in the baggage hall if you need help'.

The baggage hall is bright and airy with plants sponsored by the airline. Aircrew are there to introduce ground staff. Music is playing. You can buy toothpaste. There are clean toilets. Notices give advice on onward travel and the currency exchange sells packs of low-denomination notes and coins in the local currency.

How much better is the strong finish!

Researching a strong finish

I conducted some service research to test out my hypothesis that a strong finish makes a difference. The methodology emulated the work of Hansen and Danaher published in the *Journal of Service Research* (1999). These service researchers used a scenario methodology whereby they gave participants multiple scenarios to read and a questionnaire to complete measuring service quality judgements and purchase intentions using Likert scale responses. The scenario options offered in the Hansen and Danaher study were combinations of good or bad starts and good or bad finishes.

Building on this, my methodology employed the same approach adding a short qualitative element to the questionnaire. There were four sets of scenarios covering a range of different service types, namely mass service, catering, medical treatment and professional services. Each scenario had two versions representing a good start and a good finish – 'consistent', and a good start and an excellent close – 'strong finish'. Each participant responded to two sets of scenarios (four scenarios in total). Their responses to the scenarios were measured using the same questions and Likert scale outlined in Hansen and Danaher (1999).

I found that the 'strong finish' version scored significantly higher in all dimensions of excellent service. Customers rated the 'strong finish' significantly higher for quality and customer satisfaction. In addition, their likelihood of returning and propensity to recommend were also significantly higher for the 'strong finish'.

> in a competitive service environment a good start and a good finish are not enough

So this research evidence supports the idea that in a competitive service environment a good start and a good finish are not enough, and a strong finish can make a crucial difference.

Not with a bang but with a whimper

Of course a weak finish is bound to be damaging to the service encounter. No service strategist would plan for the ending to be the least impressive part of the experience. Yet somehow, by default, the outcomes disappoint, as in the example below.

Web-designers are proud of their efforts to create a unique and impressive home page. It is the page that everyone checks. Less time is spent on subsequent pages and the lower level pages deep in the navigation architecture never benefit from the same quality investment. Standards decay. Errors appear. Figures and illustrations fall out of date. This is how websites give a great first impression and end with a weak finish.

The warmth of the greeting to guests at the Sheraton Park Towers in Buenos Aires demonstrates textbook excellence. It is another story at the end of the stay, when the hall porters lead you to your departing taxi and bar your way into the car, with a hand out for a gratuity!

The electrical retail store environment is modern, lively and attractive. The latest merchandise is well displayed. The store sales people are well informed. But it takes ten minutes of waiting to discover that the display item is out of stock …

The bank has an impressive frontage; the lighting and ambience are professional. The banking officer suggests coffee as you discuss the car purchase. You anticipate being a car owner for the first time. All the forms and procedures are explained and the final check is a car-loan credit-score that rejects you …

Professional people handle the consulting contract. The initial report assesses the issues with candour and new insight. Contact is quick and efficient. An implementation plan is presented that addresses the challenges. But the invoice is sent to the wrong location and includes an accidental over-charge …

The patient is cured. The nurses have made the treatment as pleasant as possible. The ward is clean and bright. Dignity and privacy have been upheld. The doctor has explained everything in clear language. She has signed the discharge. And then the patient waits six hours for drugs from the pharmacy …

Managing a great ending

On the other hand, some businesses come out strongly at the end.

The restaurant waiter in the Café Jeera, who gives a good finishing touch – a chocolate and liquorice assortment with the bill. This kind of close increases five-fold the chance of a generous tip.

Ryanair pilots who sound a fanfare on landing to signal an on-time arrival (and make it very clear in their publicity that the airport is not their responsibility).

The music, DVD and game store HMV who always give you time to put away your credit card and receipt slip before handing your purchase to you. This is in contrast with other retailers who give you card, slip and purchase altogether. With two hands and three items, it is frustratingly easy for one of the three to be dropped.

Hyundai in USA, who from February 2009, will sell you a new car and then, as you drive away, give you the reassurance that if you lose your job in next 12 months, you can bring your new car back for a full refund. Do not worry about the economy – just enjoy the car.

First Great Western who end your stressful week with a complimentary Friday night glass of wine for first class ticket-holders.

Mr Frost the chimney sweep who tells you it brings good luck to see the brush head atop the chimney and takes you outside to show it.

Jessica from LK Bennett who adds a handwritten note when she mails a dress to a customer, offering to handle any problems or queries, adding in a postscript the date the next sale begins.

Architectural practice, Anderson Orr of Wheatley, Oxford who undertake commissions to secure planning permission for clients and, through imaginative and thoughtful house designs, create more value than the clients expected.

The Safari ward at Hemel Hempstead hospital has a strong finishing touch. My son had an outpatient operation to treat persistent nosebleeds on a Wednesday. Two days later, on the Friday afternoon, just after 5.00 p.m., a nurse phoned to check that the recovery was going well and ask after the patient's well-being, offering a phone number if any further concerns arose.

Prêt a Manger sandwich servers close the encounter with three specific actions. These simple but effective instructions achieve a strong finish. Put the change directly in the customer's hand (rather than tossing it on the counter), secondly look the customer in the eye and finally say something. The final words can be a thank you, a farewell, a comment on the weather or today's news, or any topic that comes to mind (see Figure A8.3). Complete all three actions and a customer will be happy. Or, if the 'customer' happens to be a mystery shopper, the server could receive an instant cash bonus for their team!

> **Hand:** put the change into the customer's hand
>
> **Eye:** look the customer in the eye
>
> **Mouth:** say something as you say goodbye to the customer

FIGURE A8.3 The three-stage farewell

Nine directions to achieve the finishing touch

There are nine techniques that influence final customer perceptions of the service they have experienced. Some are simple, some more substantive, but each can be used to good effect in service encounters, at the end of a phone call or meeting with a customer, or in the final review of a long-term customer service project.

1 Appreciation

Find a way of saying thank you after a transaction, to show you do not take their business for granted. Vary the forms of words to different customers to avoid the robotic effect of over-repeated phrases. For some customers a formal 'Thank you for your business' works better. For others, a less formal 'Thanks for the call' meets the need. To regular buyers of gardening offers, the *Daily Telegraph* sent a thank you gift of a pair of gardening gloves. The response was very positive – some readers even sent back photos of themselves wearing the gloves in their garden.

2 Senior level recognition

The thank you or the farewell can be endorsed by the presence of a senior manager. It carries weight if a board member recognises the quality or durability of the relationship. In professional services firms involve one of the partners in the sign-off at the conclusion of a project.

3 Convenience

Saving customers time and trouble makes a valuable finish. For example, at the end of a phone call or a meeting, check that there is nothing else on the customer's action list. The phone bank First Direct always ask, 'And is there anything else you need to cover today?'

4 Involvement

Where the end of the process seems to feel negative, or the customer is passive, redesign the close to increase the customer involvement. For example, in supermarket shopping the queue is a negative ending, it feels slow and the customer will begin to think about the next activity. The enforced downtime is resented. Self-scanning is a possible solution: it absorbs the full attention of the consumer so he or she cannot think about the next activity. This involvement means that this system is perceived to be faster (even if it is not).

> redesign the close to increase the customer involvement

5 Reassurance of a good choice

Congratulate the customer on a wise decision. Take care that this approach is not seen as superficial. To be credible this needs to be supported with evidence. You might for example reassure by saying that a number of other customers have bought the same item recently; in other words – you are in good company. In a business-to-business context, the close could highlight that a major company has specified the same service package.

6 A positive surprise!

Reserve a piece of good news for the final moments. For instance, provide an extra customer benefit such as a sample of a new product or an offer for next season. Or give some more general good news, that the firm has won an award. The good news could be less direct – for example, a sales agent could share the good news that she is being promoted. The company Driver's Dream Days provide experiences like driving an Aston Martin on a racetrack. As a finishing touch, they add an additional and unexpected driving thrill – a 4 × 4 Land Rover trip on a mud track – after the last item on the programme card has been completed.

7 Celebration

Identify a reason to celebrate – it is the tenth year of renewal, the 100th contract, the founder's birthday. For firms who use date of birth as a security check, consider adding a greeting in the month that the birthday occurs.

8 Positive reinforcement

Happiness research has shown that scores are higher when the sun is shining. On sunny days draw attention to the good weather as the customer is leaving. Use a positive phrase like 'Enjoy the sunshine!' Or find a current good news story or another current reason to be positive.

9 It's a pleasure to serve you

Research and implement words, actions, expressions and behaviours to illustrate that front-line people enjoy serving customers, particularly this customer. A genuine smile, as you say goodbye, can be heard in the intonation of the voice. You cannot fake a smile on the phone. The manager's role is to keep the serving staff smiling. Where staff experience a bad encounter with a rude or abusive customer, it may be necessary to allow 'emotional recovery time' in order to be able to respond positively to the next customer.

Encourage servers to use upbeat and positive expressions rather than negative phrases. Contrast the words 'no worries' with 'it is a pleasure!'

Putting it into practice

Each service business has its own unique characteristics. Different types of customers deserve and expect appropriate variations to appeal to their needs. There is no single answer across all services. Some techniques will fit with one service brand; others will jar or conflict with the service proposition. Businesses must craft a blueprint to develop their own finishing touch using the model shown in Figure A8.4.

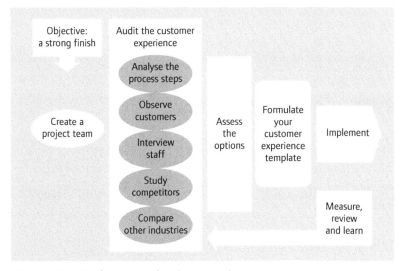

FIGURE A8.4 Crafting your finishing touch

The objective is to ensure that customers receive a strong finish to their service experience. The primary task is to develop, test and implement ideas to provide the finishing touch. A second strand is to create a process that continually reviews and enhances the finish. In this way, returning customers will find their experience keeps getting better and better.

Step 1: Create a project team

Define the project focus as the progressive and systematic build-up to the final moments of the encounter.

The project team should include members with a strategic perspective and some front-liners with current practical knowledge. It should feature a long-service employee who has seen the evolution of customer needs over time plus a member with an external viewpoint who can challenge conventional thinking. Select a mix of young and old, male and female, senior and junior, creative and practical, to secure diverse viewpoints.

After the initial report and implementation, the project team can become a steering group to keep the customer experience strong. As such, it will be necessary to replace people or co-opt new members for a flow of new approaches.

Step 2: Audit the customer experience

Research and gather data about the process

Begin by mapping stages that the customers progress through, from pre-service where needs arise and expectations are formed, all the way to post-service impressions.

- Consider all the steps of the service process: which impact most on final outcomes?
- What is the routine timescale? What are the fastest and slowest timings?
- Where are the delays and frustrations?
- Where and why are customers waiting?
- Where are the high spots?
- How are expectations set? What promises are we making?

Understand the customers

The process begins with a clear statement of customer needs and expectations. This may be straightforward where requirements are homogenous and a single consistent approach can be provided. In other businesses, the answer may be uniquely tailored to every customer individually. Or there may be clusters of needs resulting in a number of customer segments. In this case, a different approach could be required for each segment. Provide special packages or pathways for each segment. Figure A8.5 illustrates how a busy and confident customer needs different treatment from a slower and reflective buyer and be different again from a nervous novice.

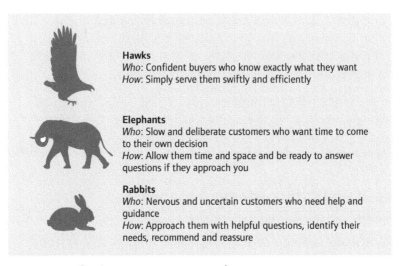

Hawks
Who: Confident buyers who know exactly what they want
How: Simply serve them swiftly and efficiently

Elephants
Who: Slow and deliberate customers who want time to come to their own decision
How: Allow them time and space and be ready to answer questions if they approach you

Rabbits
Who: Nervous and uncertain customers who need help and guidance
How: Approach them with helpful questions, identify their needs, recommend and reassure

FIGURE A8.5 Service: a segment approach

Study customers

Observe customers through the entire transaction or encounter, focusing especially on the build-up to the final elements. Interview sample customers immediately at the end of the service. Try focus groups and in-depth individual interviews. Questions to stimulate ideas include:

▌ What was the high spot of the experience?

▌ How did you feel as the service encounter came to a close?

▌ What appealed to you about the ending?

▌ What disappointed you?

▌ What could have raised the ending still further?

▌ Who does it better?

▌ What finishing touches would you like to see?

Interview staff

Invite front-line staff to give their opinions on the customer experience and what – in their view – will encourage customers to emerge on a high note.

▌ What has caused customers to complain or compliment you?

▌ When do customers smile and laugh, when do they look sombre or unhappy?

▌ What are customers saying at the end of the encounter?

▌ What expectations do customers have? What surprises them?

▌ How do you handle delays and the unexpected?

▌ What can improve a customer's mood?

▌ What have you done to help customers finish on a high note?

Study competitors

Consider the significant rivals, if the customer chose to meet his/ her needs elsewhere. Preferably study a mainstream head-to-head competitor and also a small aggressive 'piranha' type rival. You learn different things from their different positioning in the market. If possible, experience competitor service and note how they manage the experience and bring it to a close. If it is practicable, interview customers who have used your service *and* that of a competitor to check their relative perceptions.

▌ How do competitors sequence the aspects of the service?

▌ How do they manage the time of the customer?

▌ What are the high spots and how are they achieved?

▌ What are the low spots and how were they brought about? How do they recover from problems?

▌ What do they do differently and how do customers feel about this?

▌ What do the competitors do better to close the experience positively?

Study service icons from other industries

Top performers may learn little from other players in their sector. For this reason they are advised to look at alternative industries for inspiration. Consider your customers: what other services do they require and which industries serve them? What are the critical characteristics of your services and what other sectors have similar characteristics? Look at related markets and identify the lead businesses.

▌ What do they do well? How do they influence the perceptions of customers at each stage?

▌ What techniques or approaches or phrases succeed for them?

▌ How could you translate, refine and apply the ideas to your business?

Step 3: Assess and evaluate the options

This is the analytical process that reviews and filters the ideas and approaches that have emerged from the data-gathering.

▌ List all the good news and positive angles that emerge from each of the studies. Where and when are you winning? How can you make winning situations occur more frequently? How can you build on these?

▌ List all the irritants, shortfalls and problems that can arise. What lies behind them? How can you prevent or foresee these circumstances? What actions may mitigate the effects? What systems or training can prevent and/or recover the situation?

▌ Capture all the creative ideas for building a positive trajectory, and those that can prevent/reverse a decline in customer motivation. What insights can be gleaned from these findings? Develop hypotheses about what customers enjoy, what they hate, what makes them positive and what irritates or depresses them.

▌ Test your hypotheses on a representative sample of customers. Make changes in one location or with one tranche of customers. Monitor the results and compare with a control group in another location. This procedure determines the value conversion from the enhancements. What investment is required and what will be the payback? Are you gaining additional return or a competitive advantage? Where is the additional care and attention justified? Should it be applied to all customers or reserved for certain vulnerable or valuable sub-sets?

Step 4: Formulate your customer experience template

Determine a customer experience strategy. For every stage on the customer journey from pre-service to post-service (see Figure A8.6), what should be the ideal experience and what should be their feelings, perceptions and customer emotions at each point?

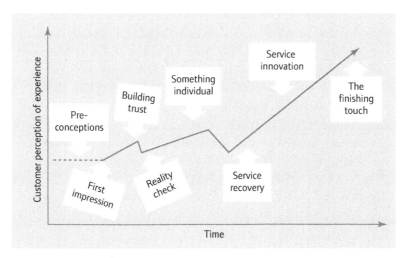

FIGURE A8.6 Satisfaction curve

Consider re-sequencing the service experience: are there pleasant aspects that can be scheduled later? Are there problems that can be eliminated, or addressed earlier in the process? Can the awkward parts of the process be simplified or amalgamated? How should you reach the grand finale?

Preconceptions

consider how to set realistic expectations

Expectation management is the focused approach to ensuring that potential customers begin to form accurate and attractive perceptions of a service and the brand's ways of working even before they have any direct contact. Consider how to set realistic expectations. Decide what you will promise through advertising and communications. Assess the signals conveyed by premises, people, uniforms, facilities and vehicles. Identify the evidence needed to persuade media commentators to convey more favourable opinions. Develop a strategy to influence word-of-mouth messages communicated by existing customers.

First impressions

There is only one chance to make a first impression. Manage the tangible signs as new customers approach your business for the first time. Consider what impression your brand aims to convey and ensure that this message is signalled through all the senses – visually, audibly, through touch and smell. Determine the style of greeting that will establish the desired impression. Train for consistent performance, measure and reward results. Focus on the actions and words that set the correct expectations. Devise a customer induction – a way of communicating the information a new customer needs to know to gain the most effective service.

Building trust

Trust is the foundation of confidence. Identify and manage the small practical steps that inculcate the trust of new customers. Ensure that words, promises and actions consistently provide the signals and evidence that customers are right to put their faith in your firm.

Checking expectations

Carry out a reality check early in the encounter to prevent a gap appearing between customer expectations and your delivery. Correct any misunderstandings about product quality, service standards or timing. In particular understand the duration and nature of customer queues or waiting. There are techniques to manage the experience and perceptions of customers as they wait. Best practices can impact on callers holding on for phone service. Enhance overall impressions by clustering any difficulties and bad news together. Assess the impact of one customer on another and encourage consideration for others.

Something individual

Every customer wants to feel important. Avoid procedures that make customers feel unimportant. Use proven techniques to make customers feel individual and special.

Service recovery

Most customers have experienced poor responses to service shortfalls. They therefore rate a convincing recovery very highly. Establish early warning devices for impending problems. Monitor, measure and enhance your recovery techniques. Develop your version of a world-class recovery.

Service innovation

The essence of good service is consistent reliability and great service providers successfully target customer perceptions every time. However, eventually customers may fail to notice good service, taking it for granted. The answer is service innovation. Scour the world for insights. Develop new value propositions. Pilot concepts with customers and learn from the feedback. Roll out the new propositions with confidence.

The finishing touch

Create the finishing touches that leave customers feeling positive, willing to speak favourably and wanting to repeat the experience. Design the blueprint for the final minute of a phone call, the final ten-minutes of a journey, the final week of a contract. Aim for every customer experience to end on a high note.

Step 5: Implement

Put the customer experience template into practice. This may require resources in terms of investment in facilities, equipment and systems. Once the hardware is available, team training will be necessary to instil or update staff behaviours towards customers. A good practice is to create a model location where trainees themselves receive the experience that is to become the model for customers.

Step 6: Measure, review and learn

Measurement is the surest way to reinforce existing good practices and change negative ones. What gets measured gets done. American Express pays staff incentives based on customer satisfaction scores. In September 2009, American Express was ranked highest for the third consecutive year in the JD Power and Associates study of 21 credit card issuers in the USA. The focus on customer satisfaction measures led the firm to innovate in the light of harsher economic circumstances. For example, Amex introduced special payment programmes for card members facing temporary financial difficulties and also enhanced the American Express website with online financial management tools, tips and advice.

> measurement is the surest way to reinforce
> existing good practices and change negative ones

UK car repair operation Kwik-Fit follows up customer visits to its automotive centres with a phone survey, funded by insurance sales made to satisfied customers. Kwik-Fit won the *Business Car* magazine award for fast-fit for the 16th year in a row in January 2009. Prêt a Manger uses mystery shoppers who give motivational bonuses to shops providing high standards of service.

Oxford-based legal firm, Henmans LLP, survey clients at the completion of a piece of work as part of an ongoing review of client care policies and procedures. Key questions focus on the overall level of service, how easy to understand was the information and advice, how well they keep clients up-to-date with progress and the likelihood of recommendation. In addition they invite comments that could help and improve the levels of service. The client questionnaire is succinct, clear and set out on a single page. In itself the clarity of the survey document reflects well on the firm.

We will end this chapter with some conclusions on measurement.

More feedback is better

Make it easy for customers to respond so that high proportions of customers give feedback and give you more valid results. I had occasion to call at the Rothersthorpe Motorway Services on the M1 motorway. The toilets were astonishingly clean – they sparkled and I wondered how this could be. On the wall as I left the toilets there were cartoon faces. If you found the toilets dirty you pressed the unhappy face. I pressed the smiley face and a recorded voice thanked me.

Timing influences results

Measurements taken immediately after the event are likely to be more positive than responses received later. Fresh feedback is usually richer than information gained some time after the purchase.

Watch for distortion

Measurement can distort behaviour, however, unless the right aspects are monitored. For example, when call centre agents are measured on the percentage of calls answered (PCA) within 20 seconds, if more calls are coming in, there is an incentive to hurry the current caller off the line. Otherwise targets and bonuses will be missed. Speed is easy to monitor, but in reality customers rate having their query answered in a single call higher than being answered in less than 20 seconds. Shaw and Ivens (2002) cite the example of T-Mobile moving from PCA as a primary measure to first call resolution.

Less is more

Measuring too many aspects can diminish impact. Effective results come from focusing on a small number of priorities. Rather than creating an extended wish list of desired behaviours, it is better to identify one key parameter for focused attention. For example, a firm might identify that error-free invoices were a key influencer on customer perceptions. With this in mind, current performance forms a benchmark and account teams are supported, trained and monitored for improvement. When scores increase, a new priority is established.

> effective results come from focusing on a small number of priorities

Measure recommendation: the net promoter score

Satisfaction alone may be insufficient to earn repeat business. When customers are truly delighted with a service they will speak positively to friends and colleagues. Fred Reichheld, working with Bain & Company, has devised a relative measure for a company's recommendation levels. Just as net worth represents the difference between financial assets and liabilities, net promoter quantifies the difference between customer assets and liabilities. With a question about willingness to recommend (on a 1–10 scale), customers can be placed in one of three categories: high-scoring *promoters* who are loyal and enthusiastic; moderate-scoring *passives* who are satisfied but unenthusiastic; and low-scoring *detractors* who are unhappy but trapped in a bad customer relationship. The net promoter score (NPS) is calculated by setting aside the passives (who have no impact on recommendation, being neither positive nor negative) and deducting the percentage of detractors from the percentage of promoters. The NPS shows the percentage by which positive recommenders outweigh customers who feel negatively about a company. It is a simple and easily communicated measure. It is also a lever for improvement. Firstly, it identifies detractors whose concerns and opinions can be addressed. Secondly, it encourages employees to focus on actions that lead customers to recommend. A strong finishing touch can be an outcome.

Measure the finish

Monitor customer opinions and feedback to the end of the process. For example, a key part of the Amazon service is the delivery. Amazon has extended its offer to include goods shipped by merchants other than themselves. Hence it is necessary to measure their performance lest poor service damage the Amazon brand experience and reputation. Amazon encourages customers to rate their experience with merchants, in the same way as eBay merchants receive scores from buyers. In addition, Amazon merchants are required to communicate with customers via the Amazon email system so that customer conversations can be subject to a spot-check. Amazon monitors orders cancelled because of stock shortages and customer complaints. Problems with more than 1% of shipments can result in merchants being delisted. The finish is vital.

Sleep Country Canada

Christine Magee, president of Sleep Country Canada, the mattress experts, received this letter from a customer, praising the company's excellent service and its powerful finishing touch:

Dear Christine:

Actually, I do not feel that I am writing a business letter but rather a letter to a friend. It is sooooo refreshing in this day and age of technology to feel as if you have received the personal touch. From the moment I walked into the store until I received my delivery I felt that your advertisement was more than you claim. I felt part of a team that wanted to ensure that I received complete satisfaction. I dealt with a team where each member was an integral part of the complete package.

Chris was very knowledgeable, friendly and I didn't feel pressured. I was given all the time I needed to test each bed to make sure I was choosing the right mattress for my needs. When Kevin phoned me with my 3-hour window they were earlier than they said. (And oh yes, those little booties, ... Kevin even pointed out to one of the guys that his was falling off. Impressive!) Unfortunately, my transaction didn't go smoothly. I ordered complete sets of box springs and mattresses for 1 queen bed, 1 double bed and 2 twin beds. Upon delivery, I got 3 double box springs instead. Even though I told Kevin that I wasn't in a hurry for the twin box springs, he insisted that what I ordered I would get today. He phoned all around to see if he could get me what I ordered but to no avail. So he drove to the nearest store and I have loaners until I receive what I ordered.

My delivery date was the day after the big snow fall, Fri Mar. 2nd. When they arrived I was outside shoveling my driveway. After they left I went back outside to resume shoveling and I found that my driveway was finished. My neighbor was outside shoveling his driveway so I thanked him for finishing mine. He informed me that one of the Sleep Country guys finished it. So thanks to either Brad or Scott for going above and beyond the call of duty.

▶

I firmly believe in Public Relations and also believe that a lot of business is obtained from satisfied customers. I have been 'good-mouthing' your company to everyone I can and I am so in awe of the personalized attention and feeling of complete satisfaction that I have received. Be assured that I will only be buying mattress sets from Sleep Country from now on. So, thank-you Christine for living up to your advertisement.

Sincerely, a more than satisfied customer.
Judy Fenton

Reproduced by permission of Sleep Country Canada,
www.sleepcountry.ca

HOW TO APPLY

The finishing touch: leaving your customers wanting more

APPLICATION: MASS SERVICE

Airlines, banks, hotels, logistics firms, retailing, train-operating companies

In mass service each customer is just one among many. Yet it is still possible to make a customer feel individual, special and positive. Set standards for the staff member who has the final piece of contact and check: did the staff member smile, make eye contact and thank the customer?

Make it positive by drawing attention to good availability, good fortune, on-time arrival or any other successful outcome.

The ending is extremely important.

Hospitals, car repairers and travel agents

The service shop is a more personalised service. Many patients and customers go through the service shop yet each one has an individual situation. Look carefully at customising the last point of contact – the travel documents, the stamp in the car service book. Impress at the final stage.

For a hospital, look carefully at the discharge notes. They can be read and re-read and leave a lasting impression – this should be positive and carry a perception of continuing care. Discharge notes are especially important where non-native English-speaking patients rely on family or friends to translate. Connect effectively with community doctors and general practitioners.

The experience is often long remembered. It is important that first-timers will recall a good result. For example, the memory of a first international trip will be recalled for a lifetime. Children will remember a stay in hospital for their whole lives. Make sure it ends with an experience that is positive.

Accountants, architects, consultants, doctors, lawyers

This is an individual service, tailored to the client, who is investing time and reputation in a professional provider. Expectations are high and the final stage is the last point to ensure that all is well and that memories are so positive that the client will recommend and return.

part

3

Epilogue

Finale

Picture the industrial scales calibrator checking the accuracy of the commercial balance, certifying it and finally leaving a demonstration of balance accuracy by placing a 200 g weight on one tray and a 200 g bar of chocolate on the other.

The customer service finishing touch is like the last dab of paint that creates the masterpiece. Hear the final high note flourish in a piece of music. It is the crescendo that leaves them wanting an encore, feeling good and eager to share the experience with others.

The ending creates a rosy glow of positive retrospection. The peaks are recalled, the troughs seem immaterial and the final ending triumphs.

It's the finishing touch.

Further reading

Chapter 1

Chase, R.B. and Dasu, S., 'Want to perfect your service? Use behavioural science', *Harvard Business Review*, June 2001, pp. 79–84

Cram, T., *Customers that Count: How to Build Living Relationships with Your Most Valuable Customers*, Financial Times Prentice Hall, 2001, chs 3 and 4

Croft, M. 'Unchartered territory', *The Marketer*, November 2006, pp. 6–9

Edgeworth, F.Y., *Mathematical Psychics: An Essay on the Application of Mathematics to the Moral Sciences*, C Kegan Paul and Co, 1881

Edwards, H., 'Customer service under the microscope', *Marketing Magazine,* 8 November 2006

Gale, B., *Monitoring Customer Satisfaction and Market-perceived Quality*, American Marketing Association: Worth Repeating Series no. 922CS01, 1992

Grove, S.J. and Fisk, R.P., 'Service theatre: an analytical framework for services marketing', in *Services Marketing,* 4th edition, Lovelock, C. (ed.), Prentice Hall, 2001, pp. 83–92

Hansen, D.E. and Danaher, P.J., 'Inconsistent performance during the service encounter – what's a good start worth?', *Journal of Service Research,* February 1999, pp. 227–235

Julius, D. and Butler, J., 'Inflation and growth in a service economy', *Bank of England Quarterly Bulletin*, November 1998, pp. 338–346

Parasuraman, A., Zeithaml, V.A. and Berry, L.L., 'SERVQUAL: a multiple item scale for measuring consumer perceptions of service quality', *Journal of Retailing*, vol. 64, Spring 1988, pp. 12–40

Reichheld, F. and Sasser Jr., W.E., 'Zero defections: quality comes to services', *Harvard Business Review*, September–October 1990, pp. 105–111

The Economist, 2006a 'Are you being served? – China', 14 January 2006

The Economist, 2006b 'Economics discovers its feelings – not quite as dismal as it was', 23 December 2006

Verhoef, P.C., Antonides, G. and de Hoog, A.N., 'Service encounters as a sequence of events', *Journal of Service Research*, August 2004, pp. 53–64

Zeithaml, V.A. and Bitner, M.J. *Services Marketing: Integrating Customer Focus Across the Firm*, McGraw Hill Irwin, 2003, ch 17, 'The financial and economic effect of service'

American Customer satisfaction index: **www.theacsi.org**

British Standards: **www.bsi-uk.com**

PricewaterhouseCoopers: **www.pwc.co.uk**

Research Now: **www.researchnow.co.uk**

UK government statistics: **www.statistics.gov.uk**

Chapter 2

Cram, T., 'Seven of the best', *Directions – the Ashridge Journal*, Summer 2003, pp. 24–28

Cram, T., *Smarter Pricing: How to capture more value in your market*, Financial Times Prentice Hall, 2006

Fitzsimmons, J.A. and Fitzsimmons, M.J., *Service Management*, McGraw Hill, 2004, see ch.5 for the Enterprise Rent-A-Car case

Grove, S.J. and Fisk R.P., 'Service theatre: an analytical framework for services marketing' in *Services Marketing,* 4th edition, Lovelock, C. (ed.), Prentice Hall, 2001

Hemp, P., 'My week as a room service waiter at the Ritz', *Harvard Business Review*, June 2002, pp. 4–11

Heskett, J.L. Sasser, W.E. and Hart, C.W.L., *Service Breakthroughs*, The Free Press, 1990, pp. 164–174

Heskett, J.L., Jones, T.O., Loveman, G.W., Sasser, W.E. and Schlesinger, L.A., 'Putting the service profit chain to work', *Harvard Business Review*, March–April 1994

Lanning, M.J., *Delivering Profitable Value: A revolutionary framework to accelerate growth, generate wealth, and rediscover the heart of business*, Capstone, 1998

Lawler, E., *Lessons in Service from Charlie Trotter*, Ten Speed Press, 2001

Mitchell, C., 'Selling the brand inside – you tell customers what makes you great, do your employees know?', *Harvard Business Review*, January 2002, pp. 5–11

Reichheld, F., *Loyalty Rules! How Today's Leaders Build Lasting Relationships*, Harvard Business School Press, 2001

Schlesinger, L.A. and Heskett, J.L., 'Breaking the cycle of failure in services', *Sloan Management Review*, Spring 1991, pp. 17–28

Shaw, C. and Ivens, J., *Building Great Customer Experiences*, Palgrave MacMillan (2002), see especially ch 6, People

Smith, S. and Wheeler, J., *Managing the Customer Experience*, Financial Times Prentice Hall, 2002

Enterprise Rent-A-Car: **www.erac.com**

Act 1

Advertising Standards Authority Reports, 2005, 2008

Gladwell, M., *The Tipping Point*, Abacus, 2002

Grove, S.J. and Fisk, R.P., 'Service theatre: an analytical framework for services marketing' in *Services Marketing*, 4th edition, Lovelock, C. (ed.), Prentice Hall, 2001, pp. 83–92

Lawler, E., *Lessons in Service from Charlie Trotter*, Ten Speed Press, 2001

Seiders, K., Berry, L., and Gresham, L.G., 'Attention retailers! How convenient is your convenience strategy?' *Sloan Management Review*, Spring 2000, pp. 79–89

Sernovitz, A., *How Smart Companies Get People Talking*, Kaplan Business, 2006

Silvestro, R., Fitzgerald, L., Johnston, R. and Voss, C., 'Towards a classification of service processes', *International Journal of Service Industry Management*, vol. 3, no. 3, 1992, pp. 62–75

Smith, S. and Wheeler, J. *Managing the Customer Experience*, 2002

Accenture: **www.accenture.com**

B&Q: **www.diy.com**

Otter Tail Power Company: **www.otpco.com**

Prestige and Performance Cars, Uxbridge: **www.911virgin.com**

Act 2

Anderson, K. and Zemke, R., *Delivering Knock Your Socks Off Service*, AMACOM, 1998

Berry, L.L., Seiders, K. and Grewal, D., 'Understanding service convenience', *Journal of Marketing*, July 2002, see p. 13, 'Improving service convenience'

Fitzsimmons, J.A. and Fitzsimmons, M.J., *Service Management*, McGraw Hill, 1998, p. 324

Frei, F.X., 'Breaking the trade-off between efficiency and service', *Harvard Business Review*, November 2006, pp. 93–101, see p. 97 for the example of the Starbucks ordering procedure

Maister, D.H., 'The psychology of waiting lines', 1985, **http:// davidmaister.com/articles/5/52**

Heskett, J.L., Sasser Jr, W.E. and Schlesinger, L.A., *The Value Chain: Treat Employees like Customers and Customers Like Employees*, The Free Press, 2003

Seiders, K., Berry, L.L and Gresham, L.G., 'Attention retailers! How convenient is your convenience strategy?', *Sloan Management Review,* Spring 2000, p. 83

Smith, S. and Wheeler, J., *Managing the Customer Experience,* Financial Times Prentice Hall, 2002, p. 59

Underhill, P., Why We Buy, Texere Publishing, 2000

Zunic, L. and Zunic, N., *Contact: The First Four Minutes*, Ballantine Books, 1989

Act 3

Bell, C.R. and Bell, B.R., *Magnetic Service*, McGraw Hill, 2003

Bibb, S. and Kourdi, J., *Trust Matters for Organisational and Personal Success*, Palgrave Macmillan, 2004

Butler, J. and Keller, V., 'A better office visit for doctor and patient', *Managed Care Magazine,* vol. 8, no. 5, 1999, pp. 51–4. Reports on the research of Wendy Levinson MD

Collins, J.C. and Porras, J.I., *Built to Last: Successful Habits of Visionary Companies*, Harper Business, 1994. The Merck quote comes from an address to the Medical College of Virginia, Richmond, on 1 December 1950, see p. 48

Coulter, K.S., 'The effects of travel agent characteristics on the development of trust: a contingency view', *Journal of Travel and Tourism Marketing*, vol. 11, no. 4, 2002, pp. 67–85

Foster, P., 'Nobel Peace Prize for banker to the poor', *Daily Telegraph*, 14 October 2006, p. 14

Gladwell, M., *Blink, the Power of Thinking Without Thinking*, Penguin, 2006. Reports on the research of Wendy Levinson MD

Levesque, P., *Customer Service from the Inside Out Made Easy*, Entrepreneur Press, 2006

Levinson, W., Roter, D.L., Mullooly, J.P., Dull, V.T. and Frankel, R.M., 'The relationship with malpractice claims among primary care physicians and surgeons', *Journal of the American Medical Association*, vol. 277, no. 7, 1997, pp. 553–559

Maister, D., Green, C. and Galford, R., *The Trusted Advisor*, The Free Press, 2002, see ch. 3, Earning trust: Part two, the trust-building process

Persaud, R., 'The animal urge', *Financial Times Magazine*, 28 August 2004, pp. 23–25

Wirz, B.W. and Lihotzky, N., 'Customer retention in the B2C electronic business', *Long Range Planning*, vol. 36, 2003, pp. 517–532

World Values Survey Association: **www.worldvaluessurvey.org**

Act 4

Berry, L.L., Seiders, K. and Grewal, D., 'Understanding service convenience', *Journal of Marketing*, July 2002, pp. 1–17, see p. 3 consumer waiting

Chase, R.B. and Dasu, S., 'Want to perfect your service? Use behavioural science', *Harvard Business Review*, June 2001, pp. 79–84

Cram, T., *Smarter Pricing*, Financial Times Prentice Hall, 2006

Fitzsimmons, J.A. and Fitzsimmons, M.J. *Service Management, Operations, Strategy, Information Technology,* 6th edition, McGraw Hill, 2008

Frei, F.X. 'Breaking the trade-off between efficiency and service', *Harvard Business Review*, November 2006, pp. 93–101. Frei identifies five types of service variability and recommends steps to reduce it

Levitt, S.D. and Dubner, S.J, *Freakonomics: A Rogue Economist Explores the Hidden Side of Everything*, Allen Lane, 2005

Nelson, E., 'Big retailers try to speed up checkout lines', *Wall Street Journal*, 13 March 2000, p. B1 (supplement), B6

Norman, D.A., 'Designing waits that work', *MIT Sloan Management Review*, vol. 50, no. 4, Summer 2009, pp. 23–28

Ordonez, J., 'An efficiency drive: fast-food lanes are getting even faster', *Wall Street Journal*, 18 May 2000, pp. A1 (supplement), A10

Seiders, K., Berry, L.L. and Gresham, L.G., 'Attention retailers! How convenient is your convenience strategy?' *Sloan Management Review*, Spring 2000, pp. 79–89

Walmsley, A., 'Losing cash on delivery', *Marketing Magazine*, 5 August 2009, p. 12

Zeithaml, V.A. and Bitner, M.J., *Services Marketing: Integrating Customer Focus Across the Firm*, McGraw Hill Irwin, 2003, see ch. 14, Managing demand and capacity

Act 5

Ash, M.K., *The Mary Kay Way: Timeless Principles from America's Greatest Woman Entrepreneur*, Wiley, 2008

Firebaugh, G. and Tach, L. *Relative Income and Happiness*, American Sociological Association, 2005

Levesque, P., *Customer Service from the Inside Out Made Easy*, Entrepreneur Press, 2006

Levesque, P., *The Wow Factory: Creating a Customer Services Revolution in Your Business*, Irwin Professional Publishing, 1995

Silvester, M. and Ahmed, M., *Living Service – How to Deliver the Service of the Future Today*, Financial Times Prentice Hall, 2008

Ritz-Carlton Hotels: **www.corporate.ritzcarlton.com**

Act 6

Anderson, K. and Zemke, R., *Delivering Knock Your Socks Off Service*, AMACOM, 2006

Bell, C. R., Zemke, R. and Zielinski, D., *Managing Knock Your Socks Off Service*, 2nd edition, AMACOM, 2007

Foust, D., 'US airways: after the "Miracle on the Hudson"', *BusinessWeek*, 19 February 2009

Hart, C.W.L., Heskett, J.L and Sasser Jr., W.E., 'The profitable art of service recovery', *Harvard Business Review*, July/August 1990, pp. 148–156

Heppel, M., *Five Star Service, One Star Budget*, Pearson Prentice Hall, 2005, see pp. 49–51

Lawler, E., *Lessons in Service from Charlie Trotter*, Ten Speed Press, 2001

McCollough, M.A., Berry, L.L. and Yadav, M.S., 'An empirical investigation of customer satisfaction after service failure and recovery', *Journal of Service Research*, vol. 3, no. 2, 2000, pp. 121–137

de Matos, C.A., Henrique, J.L. and Rossi, C.A.V., 'Service recovery paradox: a meta-analysis', *Journal of Service Research*, vol. 10, no. 1, 2007, pp. 60–77

Schlesinger, L.A. and Heskett, J.L. 'Enfranchisement of service workers', *California Management Review*, vol. 33, no. 4, 1991, pp. 83–100

Seiders, K. and Berry, L.L., 'Service fairness: what it is and why it matters', *Academy of Management Executive*, vol. 12, no. 2, 1998, pp. 8–20

Shaw, C. and Ivens, J., *Building Great Customer Experiences*, Palgrave Macmillan, 2002, see p. 135

Simons Jr, J.V. and Kraus, M.E., 'An analytical approach for allocating service recovery efforts to reduce internal failures', *Journal of Service Research*, vol. 7, no. 3, 2005, pp. 277–289

Talarico, J.M., Labar, K.S. and Rubin, D.C., 'Emotional intensity predicts autobiographical memory experiences', *Memory and Cognition*, vol. 32, 2004, pp. 1118–1132

Tax, S.S. and Brown, S.W., 'Recovering and learning from service failure', *Sloan Management Review*, vol. 40, no. 1, 1998, pp. 75–88, see pp. 79

Act 7

Berry, L.L. and Lampo, S.K., 'Teaching an old service new tricks', *Journal of Service Research*, vol. 2, no. 3, 2000, pp. 265–275

Business Week, 'When service means survival', 2 March 2009, pp. 26–31. Examples of service efficiencies in BMW, Marriott, Ritz-Carlton and USAA

Dawson, N. (ed.) *Advertising Works 17*, WARC in association with the Institute of Practitioners in Advertising, 2009, see pp. 183–205 for 'How an idea made Sainsbury's great again', by Roach, T. and Mawdsley, C.

Griffin, J., *Customer Loyalty: How to Earn It, How to Keep It,* Jossey Bass, 2002

Jones, M. and Samalionis, F., 'Radical service innovation', *Business Week* (online edition), 20 October 2008, www.businessweek.com/ innovate/content/oct2008/id20081020_368485.htm. This is an edited version of Jones, M. and Samalionis, F., 'From small ideas to radical service innovation', *Design Management Review*, vol. 19, no. 1, 2008, pp. 20–27

Kim, C. and Mauborgne, R., *Blue Ocean Strategy*, Harvard Business Press, 2005

McGregor, J., 'When service means survival', *Business Week*, 2 March 2009, pp. 26–31. Information about Charles Schwab and Lexus dealer summits

Norton, M.I, '20 breakthrough ideas for 2009', *Harvard Business Review*, February 2009, pp. 19–40. A description of the Ikea effect

The Economist, Cheap but not nasty, 21 March 2009, p. 79. A description of the rise of Air Asia

Uehira, T. and Kay, C., 'Using design thinking to improve patient experience in Japanese hospitals', *Journal of Business Strategy*, vol. 30 no. 2/3, 2009, pp. 6–12

von Hippel, E., 'Lead users: a source of novel product concepts', *Management Science*, vol. 32, no. 7, 1986, pp. 791–806

Waller, M., 'If you want something done properly, then do it yourself', *The Times*, 23 February 2009, p. 48. An account of the Hoxton Hotel and Sinclair Beecham

International Customer Management Institute: **www.icmi.com**

Information on credit card satisfaction in the USA: **www.jdpower.com/ Finance/ratings/Credit-Card-Ratings**

Act 8

Business Week, 'When service means survival', 2 March 2009, pp. 26–31. Information about Amazon supplier monitors

Chase, R.B. and Dasu, S., 'Want to perfect your service? Use behavioural science', *Harvard Business Review*, June 2001, pp. 79–84

Hansen, D.E. and Danaher, P.J., 'Inconsistent performance during the service encounter: what's a good start worth?', *Journal of Service Research*, vol. 1, February 1999, pp. 227–235

Kano, N., Seraku, N., Takahashi, F. and Tsuji, S., 'Attractive quality and must-be quality', *Hinshitsu – Quality, the Journal of Japanese Society for Quality Control*, no. 14, 1984, pp. 39–48.

Reichheld, F., *The Ultimate Question*, Harvard Business School Press, 2006

Shaw, C. and Ivens, J., *Building Great Customer Experiences*, Palgrave MacMillan, 2002, see ch. 11, Targeting: driving behaviours that impact your customer experience

Smith, S. and Wheeler, J., *Managing the Customer Experience*, Financial Times Prentice Hall, 2002, see p. 109 for Prêt a Manger example

Verhoef, P.C., Antonides, G. and de Hoog, A.N., 'Service encounters as a sequence of events: the importance of peak performance', *Journal of Service Research*, August 2004, pp. 53–61

Information on awards for fast-fit service: **www.businesscar.co.uk**

Sleep Country Canada: **www.sleepcountry.ca**

Index

Comprehensive. Authoritative. Trusted.

FT Guides will tell you everything you need to know about your chosen subject area

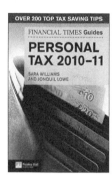

9780273735694

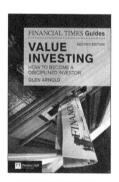

9780273724520

9780273722014

9780273729846

9780273712671

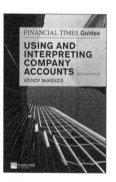

9780273723967

9780273727835

9780273740568

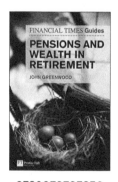

9780273727859

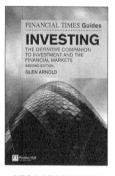

9780273723745

9780273727873

9780273729105

Change your business life today

FT Prentice Hall
FINANCIAL TIMES